Penguin Readers

ORIGINALS

ADAM GRANT

RETOLD BY NICK BULLARD

SERIES EDITOR: SORREL PITTS

Some of the quotes in this book have been simplified
for learners of English as a foreign language.

PENGUIN BOOKS

UK | USA | Canada | Ireland | Australia
India | New Zealand | South Africa

Penguin Books is part of the Penguin Random House group of companies
whose addresses can be found at global.penguinrandomhouse.com.
www.penguin.co.uk www.puffin.co.uk www.ladybird.co.uk

Originals first published in the United Kingdom by WH Allen, 2016,
and in the United States by Viking, 2016
This Penguin Readers edition published by Penguin Books Ltd, 2019

004

Original text written by Adam Grant
Text for Penguin Readers edition adapted by Nick Bullard
Text copyright © Adam Grant, 2016
Cover design by Two Associates
Cover design copyright © WH Allen, 2016

Page 15: Malcolm Gladwell, "The Sure Thing," *New Yorker*, January 18, 2010
Page 21: Ira Glass, "The Gap," accessed on April 14, 2015 at https://vimeo.com/85040589
Page 37: Coretta Scott King, *My Life with Martin Luther King, Jr.* (New York: Henry Holt & Co., 1993)
Page 44: Jessica Stillman, "Older Entrepreneurs Get a Bum Rap," *Inc.*, December 3, 2012
Page 50: Personal interview with Meredith Perry, November 13, 2014
Page 52: *The Godfather: Part II* screenplay copyright © Francis Ford Coppola
and Mario Puzo, 1974
Page 55: *The Lion King* (as *Hamlet* with lions): Personal interviews with Rob Minkoff, October 17
and November 13, 2014
Page 75: Ray Dalio, *Principles: Life and Work* (Simon and Schuster, 2017)
Page 77: Karl Weick: quoted in Robert I. Sutton, "It's Up to You to Start a Good Fight,"
Harvard Business Review, August 3, 2010
Page 86: Personal interviews with Josh Silverman, October 24, November 12, and December 2, 2014
Page 93: Interview with E.B. White by Israel Shenker, *The New York Times*, July 11, 1969

The moral right of the original author has been asserted

Printed and bound in Great Britain by Clays Ltd, Elcograf S.p.A.

A CIP catalogue record for this book is available from the British Library

ISBN: 978-0-241-39797-8

All correspondence to
Penguin Books
Penguin Random House Children's Books
80 Strand, London WC2R 0RL

MIX
Paper from
responsible sources
FSC
www.fsc.org FSC® C018179

Penguin Random House is committed to a
sustainable future for our business, our readers
and our planet. This book is made from Forest
Stewardship Council® certified paper.

Contents

Note about the book

Adam Grant was born in Michigan in 1981 and studied at Harvard University and the University of Michigan. He has a special interest in organizational psychology and is Professor of Management at the Wharton Business School of the University of Pennsylvania. Much of Adam Grant's research has been on companies in Silicon Valley, the center of American **technology*** and development near San Francisco.

This book is about **originality** and creative thinking and how they can be encouraged. It shows the many ways in which people can be successful at bringing out the most creative ideas, and how we can choose the most suitable ideas and develop them successfully.

It examines examples from the worlds of business, sports, politics, and entertainment to see what it is that makes people think originally, and how we can learn from them. It also shows how we can recognize great ideas, speak about them freely, and get other people to accept them.

Finally, it suggests a number of actions that we can take in our everyday lives to help us to develop our own originality.

*Definitions of words in **bold** can be found in the glossary on pages 109–112.

Before-reading questions

1 Think about the word "original". How would you describe a person who is original?

2 Choose the people you think will be discussed in this book.
   a Steve Jobs, the man who started Apple
   b President Barack Obama
   c Dr. Martin Luther King, Jr.
   d Jackie Robinson, the baseball player
   e Pelé, the soccer player
   f Maya Angelou, the author
   g Sherlock Holmes
   h William Shakespeare

3 Choose the products you think will be discussed in this book.
   a The Model T Ford
   b The Segway
   c The Polaroid camera
   d The telephone
   e The wireless charger
   f Skype
   g Instagram
   h The Boeing 787

CHAPTER ONE
Creativity

On a cool fall evening in 2008, four students decided to change an industry. They were all deep in debt, and they had all lost or broken their glasses. They were shocked at how much it would cost to replace them. One of them had been wearing the same pair of broken, and repaired, glasses for five years. He refused to pay for an expensive new pair.

Luxottica, the biggest company in the glasses industry, controlled more than 80% of the market. To make glasses cheaper, the four students would need to fight a giant. The four had watched Zappos change the shoe market by selling shoes online, and they wondered if they could do the same with glasses.

They discussed the idea with friends, most of whom were very negative. Nobody would buy glasses over the internet, they said. People needed to try them first. OK, Zappos had done it with shoes, but there were reasons why it wouldn't work with glasses. "If this were a good idea," people said, "someone would have done it already."

None of the students had worked in internet sales or **technology**, and they knew nothing about glasses or fashion. But they agreed to start a company. They decided to sell glasses that would cost $500 in stores for $95 online, and they would also give another pair of glasses to someone in the poorer countries in the developing world for each pair that they sold. They called their company Warby Parker.

The most important part of the business would be its website, and their Warby Parker website was ready in February 2010. They expected to sell one or two pairs of glasses a day, but in less than one month they had 20,000 customers on a waiting list.

In 2015, the magazine *Fast Company* published its yearly list of the world's most **innovative** companies. Warby Parker was the first company on that list. In the three previous years, the winners had been Google, Nike, and Apple—companies with over 50,000 **employees**. Warby Parker had just 500 employees, but in five years the company had given more than 1 million free pairs of glasses to the developing world. The company was making $100 million a year and was worth more than $1 billion.

Back in 2009, one of those four students asked me to **invest** in Warby Parker. I refused. It was the worst **financial decision** I have ever made. I needed to understand where I went wrong.

Conformity and originality

Years ago, psychologists discovered that there are two roads to success: **conformity** and **originality**. Conformity means following the crowds down the usual paths. Originality means taking unusual roads and developing new ideas that are accepted only by a few people, but that succeed in the end.

Of course, nothing is completely original: our ideas are affected by the world around us. We all borrow thoughts, sometimes by accident, sometimes not. What I mean here by "originality" is introducing and advancing an idea that is quite unusual in a particular area, and may improve that area.

Originality begins with **creativity**: having an idea that is both new and useful. But it doesn't stop there. **Originals** are people who can make their new idea really work. The Warby Parker people had the originality to think of selling glasses online, but they became originals by taking action to make those glasses cheap and easy to buy.

This book is about how we can all become more original. There's a surprising clue in the **web browser** that you use to search the internet.

The problem with defaults

In a recent research project, Michael Housman was investigating why some people who worked in customer call centers for big companies stayed in their jobs longer than others. He collected information on 30,000 employees who answered phones for banks, airlines, and cell phone companies. He expected to find that their employment histories would give him an answer. He thought people who had changed jobs often in the past would leave their present jobs more quickly. But that wasn't true.

Looking at his research, Housman noticed that his team had collected information about the internet browser that the employees had used when they applied for their job. He didn't think he would find anything interesting there, but the results were amazing. Employees who used Firefox or Chrome stayed in their jobs 15% longer than those who used Internet Explorer or Safari.

Housman thought this was strange, so then he looked at absences from work. Again, Firefox and Chrome users were 19% less **likely** to miss work than Internet Explorer and Safari users.

Then Housman looked at how employees performed in their jobs. The Firefox and Chrome users had higher sales, and their call times were shorter. Their customers were happier, too.

Housman knew it wasn't the web browser that made these people good employees. What made the difference was how they had gotten their browsers. If you buy a PC, Internet Explorer is built into Windows. If you buy a Mac, it comes with Safari. But if you choose to use Firefox or Chrome, you are not accepting the **default**.

It's the same at work. The people who didn't accept the default for their browser did their jobs differently. They didn't always accept the usual answers, and they helped their customers with new ideas.

Accepting the default is easy, but it doesn't ask us to look at new ways of doing things.

———

Before the four people behind Warby Parker started to think about their company, they knew glasses were expensive, but that had always been true. That was the default; everybody thought there was a good reason why glasses were expensive. After all, these are health products: a doctor is selling them.

Then, Dave Gilboa, one of the four, was buying an Apple iPhone. Why was this phone, a piece of modern technology, cheaper than a simple pair of glasses? Warby Parker decided to look at the glasses industry more closely. One company, Luxottica, was the biggest in the market. Simply, Luxottica could charge what it wanted: twenty **times** the cost of the glasses. And this meant that a different company could do things very differently.

Accepting defaults

We begin to accept defaults when we are very young. When researchers interviewed school teachers, they asked them to list their favorite and least favorite students. They then asked the teachers which students had the most creativity, and these were often the least favorite students. Teachers found that the creative students often made trouble, while most children learned to do what the teacher wanted.

You might think it is the most intelligent children who change the world when they become adults. But that doesn't often happen. They may become excellent doctors, but they don't ask why some people cannot afford healthcare. They may become lawyers who defend people against unfair laws, but they don't question the laws themselves. They may become teachers who teach exciting lessons but without asking what their students really need to learn.

The problem for many intelligent children is that we expect them to **achieve**. It becomes so important for them to achieve that they start to fear **failure**, which can hold back creativity.

Fear of failure held back some of the most original people in history, people who, instead of pushing ahead with **confidence**, held themselves back through fear of failure. They only took action because other people persuaded them to do so.

The men who signed the **American Declaration of Independence** were not natural **revolutionaries**. George Washington just wanted to go back to his farm and only became involved because John Adams asked him to command the army. "I have used everything in my **power** to avoid it," Washington wrote in a letter to his wife, Martha, in 1766.

Two hundred years later, Martin Luther King, Jr. wanted to work in the church and as a teacher. But, when Rosa Parks refused to give up her seat on a bus to a white man, some people in Montgomery, Alabama, decided to organize a group to support her. At a meeting, someone suggested King as president of the group. King didn't have time to think, and he accepted. He said afterward that, if he had had time to think, he would probably have refused.

When the Church asked Michelangelo to paint the ceiling of the Sistine Chapel in Rome, he wasn't interested. He didn't want to take on such a huge job and ran away to Florence. But he was asked again and again, and after two years he agreed to start work.

Nearly 500 years later, in 1977, an **investor** offered Steve Jobs and Steve Wozniak $250,000 to help them start Apple. But the investor demanded that Wozniak leave his job at Hewlett-Packard. Wozniak was afraid to leave his job, and he only agreed when he was encouraged by Steve Jobs, other friends, and his parents.

We can only wonder how many Kings, Michelangelos, and Wozniaks had original ideas but were never pushed to develop them. Many of us have ideas to improve our workplaces or schools, but we don't give voice to them. Originality can get you into trouble, and most of us prefer to **conform**.

What are the habits of people who are original, and who take action to develop their original ideas?

How to be an entrepreneur

To be an original you need to take big **risks**. That's what most people think. We admire astronauts like Neil Armstrong and Sally Ride, who left the only planet we know and went bravely into space. We admire leaders like Mahatma Gandhi and Martin Luther King, Jr., who risked their lives for the things they believed in. And we admire **entrepreneurs** like Steve Jobs and Bill Gates, who **dropped out** of school and worked in dark garages to develop the products of the future.

The word "entrepreneur" was created by Richard Cantillon, and it means someone who takes risks. When we read about the rise of Warby Parker, we see the four friends who started the company as great risk-takers. But is it true?

Six months before Warby Parker started business, Neil Blumenthal, one of the four friends, was one of my students. He came to see me because he wanted me to invest in their company. I told him that it was an interesting idea, but I wasn't sure that people would buy glasses online. As it would be difficult to persuade people to buy online, I felt it would need an enormous amount of work to get the company going. And, when I discovered what Neil and his friends were planning to do with their own lives, I was even less sure.

The first problem was that Neil and his friends were still in school. If they believed in Warby Parker, they should all drop out and work full time on Warby Parker.

"No," said Neil. "We're not sure it's a good idea, and we don't know if we will succeed. We're working on it in our spare time."

However, they were all finishing school at the end of the year.

So after that they could work full time on the project.

"No," said Neil. "If things don't work out, I'm taking a full-time job after I finish school. And so are the others."

That was enough for me. I decided not to invest. The Warby Parker friends did not fit my picture of successful entrepreneurs. They weren't prepared to risk everything on one idea. I thought they were going to fail because they didn't want any risk. But, in fact, that is why they succeeded.

———

In an interesting piece of research, Joseph Raffiee and Jie Feng studied 5,000 entrepreneurs over fourteen years. They wanted the answer to one simple question. When people start a business, is it better for them to leave their present job, or to stay employed?

If you think like most people, you would expect the risk-takers who leave their jobs to be more successful. But the opposite happens. Entrepreneurs who keep their original jobs are 33% less likely to fail than the risk-takers who leave their jobs.

If you don't like to take risks, and have some doubts about your business, you will build your business more carefully. If you take risks in your life, then you may take risks with your business, too.

Like Warby Parker, many successful businesses were started by people who did not give up their jobs—at least at the beginning. After inventing the first Apple I computer, Steve Wozniak started Apple with Steve Jobs in 1976 but continued to work for Hewlett-Packard until 1977. Larry Page and Sergey Brin developed a better way to search the internet in 1996 but didn't stop work on their higher **degrees** at Stanford University until 1998. They tried to sell

Google for less than $2 million in 1997 because their new company was making it difficult to study—luckily, nobody made an offer.

Brian May was doing a higher degree in physics when he started to play guitar in a new band. He continued to study for several years before he started to play full time for Queen. Stephen King worked in a gas station and as a teacher for seven years after writing his first story. He finally gave up work a year after his first novel, *Carrie*, was published.

These people were all balancing their risk: taking a big risk in one part of their lives but playing safe with another. Keeping things safe meant that there was space to be original. And because the entrepreneurs were not taking such a big financial risk there was more time available: there was less danger of starting the business with a poor-quality product in an effort to get the money back quickly. As Malcolm Gladwell wrote in the *New Yorker*, "Many entrepreneurs take plenty of risks—but those are generally the failed entrepreneurs, not the success stories."

From idea to action

Having revealed that successful originals often begin by questioning defaults and balancing risk, the rest of this book is about moving from original ideas to action. I have spent more than ten years researching originality and studying some of the most successful originals of our time. I want to share with you how we can all be more original, without taking too many risks with our personal, financial, and professional lives. I hope that what I have discovered will help people develop their originality and will help leaders develop originality in their organizations.

The first part of this book looks at how to manage the risks in developing, recognizing, and pushing forward original ideas. New ideas are **risky**, and we need to learn how to recognize good ideas and avoid the bad ones. Once you are sure that you have a good idea, the next step is to get other people to understand it. You'll discover how the most popular television show ever nearly didn't get made, and why an entrepreneur told investors the reasons why they shouldn't invest in his company.

The second part of this book looks at the choices we need to make when developing original ideas. There are the risks of being first to the market: it's sometimes riskier to move early than it is to be late. **Delaying** can help entrepreneurs build businesses that are stronger over time, and it can help originals remain creative. I will also look at building **coalitions** of people to work together, and how sometimes it can be useful to work with your enemies.

The third part of this book looks at how to develop originality in children and explains how our family, and others, make us more or less likely to question defaults. You'll see how whether or not baseball players are the first child in a family affects the risks that they take. I'll also look at how leaders can encourage the development of creative ideas in their companies.

To finish, I'll look at what stops us from developing our originality. The originals are the people who push us all forward. On the inside they are not that different from the rest of us. They have the same fears and doubts. What makes them different is that they try, even though they have fears and doubts. They know failure is a smaller disappointment than failing to try.

CHAPTER TWO
Ideas and inventors

Around the year 2000, a lot of people in Silicon Valley were very interested in a new **invention**. Steve Jobs said it was the most exciting technology since the computer. He offered the **inventor** $63 million to buy 10% of the company, but the inventor wasn't interested. The man behind Amazon, Jeff Bezos, told the inventor, "You have a product so revolutionary, you'll have no problem selling it."

The inventor was described as a modern Thomas Edison, and he was behind a number of exciting medical inventions. He thought his new invention would have sales of 10,000 a week in its first year. But, after six years, he had only sold 30,000, and the company still wasn't making money. The invention was expected to change lives and cities around the world, but today it is only used in a few special markets.

The revolutionary product was the Segway—a machine with two wheels that carries you around. Why did so many people think it was going to be a success? Why did they get it wrong?

A few years earlier, two writers wrote a 90-minute television program. They had never written for television before, and they soon found they didn't have enough material for 90 minutes, so they decided to write a weekly half-hour show. But when they sent their work to a television company the people there either didn't like it, or didn't understand it.

One program was made and shown to a test audience of

100 people. The viewers didn't like it. 600 more people in four different cities watched it. The report on those test audiences said: "Nobody in the audience wanted to watch the show again."

Surprisingly, the program did make it to television, and, as expected, it wasn't successful. But one person at the television company believed in it and argued that they should try making some more shows. These were made, and shown a year later, and, again, they weren't popular. The television company were going to cancel the program but agreed to do a few more shows when another program was canceled. One of the writers almost left the show—he had no more ideas.

It's a good thing he changed his mind. For the next ten years the program was one of the most popular on television, and it made more than $1 billion. *TV Guide* named it the greatest television program of all time. Why did the television companies not believe in *Seinfeld*?

When we say there is not enough originality in the world we think it is because there is not enough creativity. We think that if only people had more new ideas we would be better off. But the real problem is not new ideas—it's selecting the right ideas. Our companies and countries have many people with new ideas. What they don't have are people who can choose the right new ideas. Segway was a false positive: people thought it would be a success, but it wasn't. *Seinfeld* was a false negative: people expected it to fail, but it succeeded.

This chapter is about selecting the right ideas. We'll look at two people who did expect the Segway to fail, and at the one person in the television company who believed in *Seinfeld*. We'll see how these people made the right decisions, and how we can become better at choosing the right ideas.

Judging creativity

The inventor of the Segway was a brilliant man called Dean Kamen. He had started inventing when he was sixteen, and some of his inventions were very successful. In the 1990s, he designed the iBOT, a wheelchair that could climb stairs. He realized that the technology of the iBOT could be used more widely, and he put together a team to design the Segway. He wanted something that would be safe, friendly for the environment, and would help people to move around busy cities. Because it was small, light, and easy to ride, it would be great for mail carriers, police officers, and golfers, but it could also change the way everybody traveled. The Segway was the most amazing technology he had ever created. Kamen thought it would replace the car, in the same way that the car had replaced the horse.

But inventors are not the best people to judge their own inventions. Studies show that most of us are bad at judging ourselves. For example:

- 70% of high school seniors think they are "above **average**" leaders; 2% think they are below average
- 94% of college professors think their work is above average
- in two different companies, 32% and 42% of engineers estimated they were in the top 5% in their work.

When we have developed an idea we are usually too close to it to judge it accurately. In music, many experts think Beethoven was a good critic of his own music. But Beethoven's own favorite pieces have not been the ones played most. Aaron Kozbelt looked at letters where Beethoven judged seventy of his works and compared Beethoven's estimates with those of other experts. Of those seventy works, Beethoven estimated fifteen false positives—works that he thought were important, but that are not—and eight false negatives—works that he thought unsuccessful, but that are now judged very highly. That's 33% wrong, even though Beethoven was judging his work after audiences had heard and judged it.

Kissing frogs

If originals are not good at judging their own work, how do they create great products? They have a lot of ideas. Dean Simonton has looked at many really successful creators and discovered that they didn't have better ideas than others; they had more. By producing more ideas, they had a better chance of originality.

Think about William Shakespeare. In twenty years he wrote thirty-seven **plays** and 154 poems. In order to judge how popular they were, Simonton looked at how often the plays were performed. Three of Shakespeare's five most popular plays, *Macbeth*, *King Lear*, and *Othello*, were written in the same five years that he wrote *Timon of Athens* and *All's Well That Ends Well*, which many people feel are among the worst of his plays.

Pablo Picasso produced more than 1,800 paintings, 12,000 drawings, and thousands of other works, but only a small number of these are widely admired. Albert Einstein published 248 papers over his life, but most of them are not considered important. We know Maya Angelou's poem "Still I Rise" and her book *I Know Why the Caged Bird Sings*, but we forget about her other 165 poems and six books. If you want to be original, "the most important possible thing you could do," says Ira Glass, "is do a lot of work."

Many people think that if you want to do better work you should do less and spend time on delivering high-quality work. But having a lot of ideas is the best way to get to quality. Original thinkers will have many ideas that are of no use, but, because they develop so many ideas, it is more likely some of them will be successful.

When he was developing the Segway, Dean Kamen knew it was important to explore as many ideas as possible. "You've got to kiss a lot of frogs," he would say to his team, "before you find a prince." He encouraged them to look at hundreds of different ways of solving the problems they met. The problem was that he decided to develop the Segway without knowing whether, in the end, it would be a frog or a prince.

One of the best ways of judging our ideas is to get **feedback**. One of the writers of *The Daily Show*, Lizz Winstead, still doesn't know, after years of working on the **comedy** program, what will make people laugh. In the past she would try jokes out on stage, to an audience. Some jokes made people laugh, some didn't. Now, with social media she can get feedback more quickly. When she thinks of a joke, she shares it on Twitter. When she has something longer to share, she uses Facebook. At the end of the day, the feedback tells her whether an idea is worth developing or not.

When developing the Segway, Dean Kamen didn't look for feedback. He was afraid that somebody would steal his idea, so he kept the program secret. Many of his own employees weren't allowed to see the Segway while it was being developed. So the team working on the Segway developed a huge number of ideas, but they didn't get any feedback from customers. No customers saw it when it was being developed.

But Kamen and his team weren't the only people who were **enthusiastic** about the Segway. Why did Steve Jobs and Jeff Bezos make the same mistake? To find the answer to that question, let's first look at why so many people were wrong about *Seinfeld*.

The danger of false negatives

When the television company first looked at *Seinfeld* they didn't know what to do with it. It wasn't like other television programs. They didn't want to take a risk on something new like this. It would be better to develop a safe idea than take a risk on this new one. This way of thinking produces false negatives.

The false negative is something that happens often in the media. Film companies rejected movies like *Star Wars*, *E.T.*, and *Pulp Fiction*. Publishers refused books like *The Diary of Anne Frank*, *Gone with the Wind*, and *Harry Potter*—by 2015, J.K. Rowling's Harry Potter books had brought in over $25 billion and sold more copies than any book series ever. And in business there are hundreds of examples where employees were ordered to stop work on projects that were later successful. The Xbox was almost stopped by Microsoft, and the **laser** printer was nearly canceled by Xerox because it was too expensive.

When we see something unusual, we often refuse it and look for reasons why it may fail. When managers see something new, they compare it to things that were successful in the past. So some publishers thought *Harry Potter* was too long for a children's book. And television company managers thought *Seinfeld* was too much about New York to be of interest to the rest of the country.

Test audiences are no better than managers at judging new television shows. They make the same mistakes. When you watch a show at home, in your living room, you get interested in the story. If you laugh a lot, at the end you will think it was funny. But in a test audience you don't watch in the same way. You know you are there to judge it, and so you compare it with shows you know are funny. Neither test audiences nor managers are a good way of deciding whether a show is funny or not.

Wide experience and deep experience

When the test audiences were negative about *Seinfeld*, the project nearly stopped. But one man, Rick Ludwin, believed in it. Rick Ludwin worked on special programs, not comedy, so *Seinfeld* wasn't his department. But, because his experience was in a different type of television, he felt differently about the project. Most comedy programs before *Seinfeld* had a few complete stories, with endings, inside 22 minutes of television. *Seinfeld* started a lot more stories but sometimes didn't finish them. That worried most television managers, but Ludwin worked on specials, where each program is organized in its own way.

Ludwin had written jokes for Bob Hope in the 1970s and had worked on comedies in the past. Because Ludwin had some experience of comedy, he understood how it worked. And, although he hadn't worked in comedy for many years, he had a wide experience of television, and he was happy to explore new ways of making people laugh. He combined a wide experience of television outside of comedy with a deep experience of comedy from his days writing jokes. And combining wide and deep experience is very important for creativity.

A recent study looked at every Nobel Prize-winning scientist from 1901 to 2005 and compared them with other scientists who had not won Nobel Prizes. Both groups knew their science well—they had deep experience. But the Nobel Prize winners were more likely to be doing other, artistic, things as well. Here's what the fifteen researchers at Michigan State University found when they compared the Nobel Prize winners with the other scientists.

Artistic activity	Nobel Prize winners compared to other scientists
Music	2 times more likely
Drawing, painting, etc.	7 times more likely
Wood- or metal-working, mechanics, electronics, etc.	7.5 times more likely
Writing: poems, plays, novels, etc.	12 times more likely
Performing: acting, dancing, etc.	22 times more likely

A study of thousands of Americans showed similar results for entrepreneurs and inventors. These people were more likely than others to take part in activities like drawing, painting, or writing.

In a study of the fashion industry, a team of researchers led by Frédéric Godart looked at the cultural experience of fashion designers. The most creative work came from designers who had worked in foreign countries, but Godart found three especially interesting things about this experience.

Firstly, living in a foreign country didn't help creativity. It was working there that was important. The most original work came from designers who had worked in two or three different countries. Secondly, the more foreign the country the better. For an American, working in Canada didn't help a lot. Working in Korea or Japan helped more with originality. Thirdly, the experience was better if it was deep. A few weeks wasn't useful; the most creative designers had spent thirty-five years working in other countries.

Where Steve Jobs went wrong

When Steve Jobs first got on a Segway, he refused to climb off. When Dean Kamen wanted other investors to try it, Jobs let them, but soon got back on again. He invited Kamen to dinner and told him his Segway was as original as the computer, and he wanted to be involved.

Steve Jobs was famous for making decisions through **intuition**, rather than investigating carefully. Why did he get it wrong this time? There were three main reasons: he didn't have experience of this area of business; he felt too confident because of his success in other areas of business; and he was very enthusiastic.

Let's start with experience. Jobs and the other early investors in Segway, like Jeff Bezos, knew nothing about **transportation**. They were originals in their area, but that did not make them good in other areas. Intuition can be helpful, but it works best when we have experience of what we are looking at. The Segway was a brilliant machine, and it was huge fun to ride it. But it was difficult for people with no transportation experience to judge it.

One man who did understand the problems with Segway was Randy Komisar. He looked at the transportation market and realized that the Segway wasn't going to replace the car: it would replace walking or cycling. But he didn't think it was a product many people would want. It was exciting to ride, but it was a lot of money to pay for something that replaced walking. And, at that time, nobody knew whether governments would allow it on sidewalks. Komisar thought there would be a market in mail or police services, or for golfers. But Jobs still thought that Segway was too exciting to fail.

Jobs' next problem was that he had been very successful in one area of business, so he thought he understood all areas of business. The more successful people are in the past, the worse they perform when they work in a new area. He was so sure his intuition was right that he didn't check his intuition with people who understood transportation.

When Kamen talked with investors like Jobs about Segway, he spoke about countries like China and India, which were building cities the size of New York every year. These cities would be full of cars, and that would be really bad for the environment. He was enthusiastic, and the investors liked that **enthusiasm**. When we look at a new idea, the enthusiasm of the inventor can make a big difference. Enthusiasm is important for inventors, but entrepreneurs need to be more careful.

Thoughts on selecting ideas

My failure to invest in Warby Parker was a big false negative. I had never owned glasses, so it was hard for me to think about people who did. I had deep experience of glasses: I had spent two years doing research in a company that made and sold glasses through stores. But I didn't have wide experience. Three of the four men behind Warby Parker wore glasses, and the fourth, Neil Blumenthal, had worked for five years in Asia, Africa, and Latin America, helping women to start businesses. One of the businesses he helped with was selling glasses, so he knew that glasses could be made much more cheaply than people think.

The Warby Parker entrepreneurs were also careful to get everybody in the company involved in development. Nothing was secret, and ideas were shared on a Google document, where everybody in the company could read them. And people could give feedback on new ideas as they appeared. If Segway had done the same as Warby Parker, they may have avoided some of their problems.

But Kamen is still a great inventor, especially in the area of healthcare. As an inventor, he should be having the great ideas but then sharing them with others and getting feedback on which inventions are the most useful.

In 2013, 300,000 **patents** were taken out in the United States. The chances that any of these inventions will change the world are tiny. One creative inventor, with lots of inventions, has a better chance that one invention over his or her whole life will make a difference. And when we judge these inventors, we don't look at their least successful ones: we look at the best.

CHAPTER THREE
Speaking the truth

In the early 1990s, a **CIA (Central Intelligence Agency)** employee called Carmen Medina worked in Europe for three years. When she returned to the United States, she found that leaving the United States had made it difficult to get an interesting job in the CIA, and she began to look for other ways to help the organization.

During the time she worked for the CIA in Europe, she had noticed that there was a big problem with information sharing in the organization. Information was shared by "finished intelligence reports," which were sent out once a day. The experts who wrote them had no way of sharing ideas before the reports went out. Things change very quickly in intelligence, and it was taking too long for the right information to reach the right people. Carmen Medina suggested that, instead of using printed paper documents, departments could put their ideas immediately on to Intelink, a secret internet used by the CIA.

Her managers weren't interested. The internet was dangerous, and intelligence had to be secret. With printed documents you could be sure the right people had the right information. It would be very dangerous if the wrong people got secret information.

Medina kept talking about her idea, but everybody told her to be quiet. Finally, she decided to leave the CIA, but she couldn't find another job. She ended up working in a boring CIA desk job, and she kept quiet about her idea for a while. Three years later, she decided to argue again for online information sharing.

Less than ten years later, Carmen Medina was involved in creating Intellipedia, a Wikipedia for intelligence organizations. It allowed departments to read reports from other organizations. It was a big change to the secret culture of the CIA, and it helped with intelligence for the Beijing Olympics and after the Mumbai attacks in 2008. In a few years, Intellipedia had half a million users and over 1 million pages. It achieved this very quickly and very cheaply, too.

Why did Medina fail the first time she talked about information sharing, and why was she heard the second time? In between, the world had changed. The internet was much more widely used, and the attacks of September 11, 2001 made it clear that intelligence organizations needed to be better at sharing information. Medina had also become deputy director of intelligence at the CIA, which gave her the power to follow her idea. She got that position by learning to speak in ways that made people listen to her and believe her.

We have all sometimes wanted to speak about something that seems wrong either inside or outside of an organization. This chapter is about how to do this well, and without risks. What are the right times to speak, and how can we make sure people hear us? As well as Carmen Medina, we'll hear about an entrepreneur who tells investors why they shouldn't invest in his companies; a manager who argued with Steve Jobs; and why managers who appear to support you sometimes provide the least support. We'll also see how **gender** and **race** affect our ability to be heard, and why the photos we like of ourselves are the opposite of the ones we like of our friends.

Power without status

Leaders and managers like it when employees offer help, do research, or ask for feedback. But there's one thing that is not so popular: making **suggestions**. In one piece of research in an industry, it was found that the more employees made suggestions to their managers the less likely they were to get **promoted**.

To understand what happens in organizations when people like Carmen Medina object to something, we need to think about power and **status**. Power is being able to control what other people do; status is being admired by other people. When people without status make suggestions, we don't think they should tell us what to do, and we refuse. That is what happened to Carmen Medina; her years working outside of the United States meant she had low status. She hadn't been able to show people what she could really do, so people didn't value her ideas.

Years later, she had earned status because she had slowly gotten jobs with more responsibility in the organization. Then she got a job where she had to protect sensitive information. Now, when she talked about sharing information, it was part of her job. People saw that she stood *for* something and not *against* it. They started to admire her work, and this made it possible for her ideas to be seen as original. We don't like originality in low-status people, but we admire it when their status is high.

The Sarick Effect

After having their first child, Rufus Griscom and Alisa Volkman were shocked by the false advertising and bad advice being offered to parents. They started an online magazine called *Babble* that aimed to tell the truth about being a parent. In 2009, when Griscom tried to get investors for the project, he did the opposite to what every entrepreneur is taught to do. He told the investors the top five reasons for *not* investing in his business.

That should have killed the idea. Investors are looking for reasons to say yes, and he was giving them reasons to say no. Entrepreneurs are supposed to talk about the great things in the company, and he was doing the opposite. But it worked. That year, *Babble* got $3.3 million from investors.

Two years later, Griscom went to see Disney to see if they were interested in buying *Babble*. He did the same thing again and told them: "Here's why you should not buy *Babble*." Then he explained that people who looked at the *Babble* website didn't stay very long. And *Babble* was supposed to be for parents, but 40% of the messages people wrote on it weren't about parents at all. What's more, the technology behind the website needed some serious work. Disney bought the company, for $40 million.

This is called the Sarick Effect, after Leslie Sarick. Griscom was talking to people who had more power than him. He was asking them to give him money. Usually you would tell people what was good about your project, but that only works when people are already on your side. When you're talking to investors, they are looking for reasons why your idea won't work. In that situation it may be better to talk about what is wrong with your idea. Here are four reasons why the Sarick Effect can work.

First, beginning with what is weak about a business helps to put the audience on your side. When we know somebody is trying to push us into buying something we usually refuse. But when Griscom said the words "Here's why you shouldn't buy this company," they laughed and then relaxed. He had given them a problem to solve.

Second, talking about what is wrong with an idea makes you look intelligent. People who say and write negative things are usually seen to be more intelligent than people who say and write positive things. When you say something negative about an idea, it shows you have thought about it. In Griscom's case, it showed he knew there were problems, and he wasn't trying to hide them.

Third, talking about the problems with your business means that investors will trust you more. When Griscom talked about his problems it made him look honest. Of course, talking about the problems doesn't work if your audience doesn't know about them, but Griscom's audiences were going to give him a lot of money. They were looking at his business very carefully, so he couldn't hide the problems anyway; they would find them. Also, investors thought that, if he was admitting what was wrong with his business, there was probably a lot that was right.

Fourth, audiences are more likely to support an idea when the problems are made clear. When Griscom told investors about the problems with the business, it made it difficult for them to think of other problems with it, and they began to think that maybe Griscom's problems weren't too bad.

The unfamiliarity problem

When you have spent weeks, months, or even years thinking about your idea, you know it perfectly. It's not possible to imagine what the idea sounds like to someone who is hearing it for the first time. So we often present our ideas to people without enough information.

If we want people to accept our original ideas, we need to speak about them often, and then repeat what we said. To illustrate, which of these two words do you like better?

    iktitaf   *sarick*

If you're like most people, you will choose *sarick*.

Robert Zajonc has described this. He showed people nonsense words like *iktitaf* and *sarick* and asked them which they preferred. If they had never seen either word before, they liked them equally. But when they had seen one of the words twice before the test, they preferred that one. And if they had seen it five, ten, or twenty-five times, they liked it even more.

I used *sarick* four times earlier. There is nothing called the Sarick Effect, and there is nobody called Leslie Sarick. I invented them to show how seeing the word already can affect you. (Rufus Griscom is real, however, and so is everyone else in this book.)

My favorite test of this is when people looked at photographs of themselves and their friends. Some of the photos were inverted—as though in a mirror—and some were not. People liked the photos of their friends when they weren't inverted—because that's how they are used to seeing them. But they preferred photos of themselves that were inverted—because we're used to seeing ourselves in the mirror.

One reason for this is that the idea or picture we're used to is easier to understand. Something that we don't know takes more effort, and that makes us uncomfortable.

Making people uncomfortable

When Carmen Medina made no progress the first time she talked about information sharing, she thought about leaving the CIA. She stayed, but she didn't speak up to her managers again about her ideas for a long time. When she did it was because of her manager, Mike. I guessed Mike would be a friendly, relaxed man, but he was the opposite. He was not friendly, and he got angry quickly. So why was he the right manager for Medina?

Although he was a difficult man, Mike did care about the future of the organization. Friendly people like everyone around them to be happy, so they are less likely to push difficult ideas forward. A man like Mike didn't mind making people uncomfortable, so he was ready to give Medina time to develop her uncomfortable ideas.

Another thing that Medina noticed was that middle managers were the most unhappy with her ideas. It is often the people in the middle who don't want to make difficulties. They have made some progress in the organization and don't want to go backward.

The difficulties of speaking up

Speaking up to an audience of middle managers is always a risk, but it was especially difficult for Carmen Medina because she was a woman in an organization where most of the employees were men. I thought the days when women could not speak up in work were in the past. But I soon realized there is still a problem with gender. In organizations around the world, people expect men to speak up, and to lead. But when women speak up they can be seen as angry.

When I looked at my own research I was very disappointed. In an international bank and a healthcare company, I found that suggesting good ideas led to promotions for men, but not for women. Other research shows that male employees who talk more than others are rewarded and promoted. But women who talk more are judged negatively by both men and women. When women suggest changing something at work to improve it, their bosses don't trust them and are not as likely to change anything.

There is no doubt things were difficult for Medina because she was a woman in an organization of mostly men. But she was also a Puerto Rican. Being from two groups like this makes a difference. Ashleigh Rosette, an African-American researcher, found that people behaved differently when she spoke up than when white women and black men did. When black women leaders failed, they were judged harder than black men, or than white men and women.

The road not taken

In 1985, Donna Dubinsky was working as Apple's **distribution** and sales manager. It was a busy job, as sales of Apple computers were increasing quickly. Then Steve Jobs suggested that Apple stop using its six distribution centers and move to "just-in-time" distribution: computers would be finished in the factory when they were needed and would be delivered to customers direct from the factory.

Dubinsky thought this was a big mistake. She knew that Apple's success depended on successful distribution. She objected, but nobody listened. For several months, she worked in a group that looked at just-in-time distribution. Everyone seemed happy to go ahead with the new just-in-time **system**, except Dubinsky. She spoke up against the idea and told Apple they must give her thirty days to create a different system—and if they didn't give it to her she would leave.

She was taking a big risk, but she was given the time. At the end of the thirty days she suggested a new distribution system, and it was accepted. People knew she had done a good job in the past—she had status. Many people would think that arguing with Steve Jobs, known as a difficult man, would not be a good idea. But Jobs liked people who argued with him, and he was open to new ways of doing things. And Dubinsky wasn't doing it for herself, she was doing it for Apple. Jobs understood that.

In 1991, Dubinsky left Apple. She met Jeff Hawkins and joined Palm Computing, which produced the PalmPilot, one of the first small handheld computers. But when Palm was bought by 3Com she was again unhappy with the management. She and Hawkins left to start a new company, Handspring, which made handheld computers and developed a smartphone. A few years later, Apple developed the iPhone.

Medina had wanted to leave the CIA but couldn't. That was why she stayed and, in the end, changed the organization from the inside. Dubinsky did leave and helped to begin the smartphone revolution. Although Medina stayed and Dubinsky left, they both chose to speak up rather than remain silent.

CHAPTER FOUR

Taking time

Late at night in a hotel room, a young man stared at an empty piece of paper on the desk. Nervously, he called a friend in a room several floors down to talk through some ideas. The friend ran up the stairs to discuss a speech that would change history. At 3 a.m. the young man was still working. It was August 1963, and, although he expected to speak to 100,000 people in Washington the next day, Martin Luther King, Jr. still hadn't finished his speech.

"He worked on it all night, not sleeping," King's wife, Coretta, remembered. "He was to be the final speaker, and his words would be carried on television and radio to millions of people in America and across the world."

The speech had been announced two months earlier, and King knew how important it would be. It would only be five minutes long, so he had to be very careful in choosing his words. You might think he would begin writing the speech immediately, as soon as he knew about it. But he didn't begin writing until 10 p.m. the night before.

Parents and teachers usually ask children to begin work on their homework early, instead of waiting until the last minute. But maybe it was because King **procrastinated** that he gave the best speech of his life. I've studied originals for a long time, and I've learned that arriving early is not always a good thing. It's sometimes better to arrive at the last minute.

This chapter looks at the question of when to take original action. I'll discuss how delaying can be useful, and why procrastinating can be a good thing. I'll look at how entrepreneurs who are first to market with a product can have difficulties; why older innovators are sometimes better than younger ones; and how leaders who want to change things wait patiently for the right time. You don't have to be first to be an original; you don't even have to arrive on time. Originals are often late to the party.

Great procrastinators

Recently, a student of mine, Jihae Shin, came to me with an interesting idea: procrastinating might be good for originality. When you procrastinate you may be thinking about the thing you have to do, but you delay doing it. Shin wondered whether the delay meant that you had time to think about a number of different possibilities, rather than just one idea. As a result you may have more original ideas. I asked her to test her **theory**.

There was an empty building at college, where there had been a small food store. Shin asked students to write ideas for using the empty space. When the students started work immediately, most of their ideas weren't very original—they suggested things like another food store. But Shin asked some students to procrastinate by giving them computer games to play first. The business ideas these students produced were more original. The ideas from the **procrastinators** were 28% more original.

We were excited by these results but wondered whether playing the games had helped creativity. But when people played games *before* they were asked for ideas, it didn't help originality. It also didn't help to start work, then stop and take a break, and then return to work. Once the students had started work they had made too much progress to stop and start again. They had to know what was wanted, and to procrastinate, in order to have the most creative ideas.

Shin then did some more research, looking at a Korean furniture company. Managers thought employees who procrastinated a lot were more original than those who didn't. But procrastinating wasn't always a good thing: if the employees weren't really determined to solve a big problem, delaying just made things late. But, when they were excited about looking for new ideas, procrastination helped a lot.

Leonardo da Vinci was a famous procrastinator. Experts think he took sixteen years to paint the *Mona Lisa*, stopping and starting many times. He also spent fifteen years thinking about *The Last Supper*, working on many other things at the same time.

In American history there may be only one speech as famous as King's: Abraham Lincoln's Gettysburg Address. In just 272 words, Lincoln made clear that the Civil War was about **freedom** and **equality**. Lincoln was invited to give the speech two weeks earlier. By the day before, he had only written about half of the speech. He didn't write the last paragraph until the night before, and he didn't finish it until the morning. He waited because he wanted to be sure the speech was right.

In the summer before his "I have a dream" speech, King got advice from three people about what he should say—and how. He also discussed the speech for a long time with Clarence Jones, who had written some of his other speeches. Jones and another man began to write some ideas for the speech. King waited until the last four days before he began to work on the speech. Then, the night before, he met with his advisors, and they started again.

By delaying the work on the speech, King was giving an example of the Zeigarnik effect. The Russian psychologist Bluma Zeigarnik showed that people remember unfinished things better than finished things. Once something is finished, we stop thinking about it. But if it's not finished, it is still there in our minds. When King finally asked Jones to write the complete speech, he had a wide range of ideas. But that wasn't the only good thing about procrastinating.

"I have a dream"

Fifty years after King's famous speech, we can all remember four words: "I have a dream." I was very surprised when I looked at the speech King had written, and the words were not there. Jones didn't put them in, and King did not add them.

While he was speaking, the singer Mahalia Jackson was behind him. She shouted, "Tell them about the dream, Martin." He continued with his speech, but she shouted it again. In front of a crowd of 250,000, with millions more watching on television, King pushed his notes to one side and talked about his dream.

According to Drew Hansen in his book, *The Dream*, King was still cutting out lines and writing new ones just before he started to speak. He was even making changes as he walked up to give the speech. And he didn't read the words exactly, he changed things slightly, like a jazz musician. It was eleven minutes into the speech that he started to talk about his dream, and he added so much to the speech that he spoke for much longer than expected.

King had procrastinated, but he had given more than 350 speeches in the year before the "I have a dream" speech. He had material in his head that he could use when he needed it. He put his speeches together from pieces of all his other speeches.

Pioneers and settlers

After working on starting over one hundred new companies, Bill Gross did some research to find out why some companies succeeded and others failed. The biggest reasons were not the quality of the ideas, the people in the team, or the amount of money invested. "The number one thing was timing," Gross said. 42% of the difference between success and failure was timing.

Most Americans believe it is better to be the first mover. We want to be leaders, not followers. If you are the first to market with a new product, you can learn about the market more quickly and get the most customers. By doing that you stop the competition, because it will be hard to persuade those customers to change.

In a famous study, researchers Peter Golder and Gerard Tellis compared the success of companies that were either pioneers or settlers. Pioneers were the first movers: the first company to make or sell a product. The settlers arrived later; they waited for the pioneers to create a market first. When Golder and Tellis looked at hundreds of products in more than thirty different areas of business they found a huge difference in failures: 47% for pioneers and just 8% for settlers. And even when the pioneers did survive they only got around 10% of the market compared with 28% for settlers.

Surprisingly, the problems for the first mover are often huge. Pioneers may sometimes get a big part of the market, but they usually have a big risk of not surviving, and they often don't make much money. If you're thinking of moving into a new area of business, you need to stop and think about timing. But researcher Lisa Bolton found something more frightening. Even when entrepreneurs know it is risky to be the first mover, they don't believe it. We can all think of pioneers who succeeded, and we've forgotten those who failed. So what are the reasons that settlers do better than pioneers?

First, many people think that settlers are just copying the pioneers, but that isn't really true. They may be waiting before introducing something new. They may be working on something that is better than the products in the market now. In home video games, the pioneer was Magnavox Odyssey, which started with simple sports games in 1972. A settler, Nintendo, started to manage the distribution for Odyssey in Japan in 1975 and then, in the 1980s, started to sell the Nintendo Entertainment System, with games like *Super Mario Bros*. Nintendo's games improved on the older games; it was easier to play them, and the characters were interesting. You don't have to be first to be original. You have to be different and better.

In the 1990s, a banker, Joseph Park, was at home in his apartment. He was annoyed because he wanted to stay home and watch a movie, but to do that he had to go out to a store and rent one. Why couldn't he go to a website, choose a movie, and have it delivered to his door? As there didn't seem to be a company that provided this service, Park decided to create one.

Although Park collected $250 million from investors, his company, Kozmo, only survived until 2001. The biggest mistake was that Kozmo promised to deliver movies in one hour, and spent a lot of money on distribution to try and make that possible. If Park had moved more slowly, he might have realized that delivering movies in an hour wasn't going to work. A lot of people wanted online movies, and Netflix was just beginning. Maybe Kozmo could have competed with movies by mail, and then it might have been able to move to delivery online.

Second, it seems that people who choose to move late may be better suited to succeed. Risk-takers like to move first, and they may make their decisions too quickly. Entrepreneurs who want to avoid risk, watch the market and wait for the right time. In research into software companies, Elizabeth Pontikes and William Barnett found that when entrepreneurs waited for the market to cool down, they were more likely to succeed.

Third, as well as avoiding some risk, settlers can look at their competitors' products and make their own products better. When you are first, you have to make all the mistakes yourself. Settlers can watch you and learn from your mistakes.

Fourth, pioneers often stay with the first products they sell. Settlers can watch how the market changes and change their products so they remain right for the changing market. Settlers can also wait for the market to be ready for them. When Warby Parker started, people had been selling products online for ten years, even though the idea hadn't worked before for glasses.

The theory of pioneers and settlers is true outside of the world of business as well. In the 1840s, the Hungarian doctor

Ignaz Semmelweis discovered that if medical students washed their hands the number of women patients who died giving birth was much lower. Other doctors laughed at him. He became sick and died a young man. Twenty years later, the research of Louis Pasteur and Robert Koch showed Semmelweis to be right.

I don't want to say that it is never good to be first. If we all wait for someone else to move first, nothing original will ever be created. Someone has to be the pioneer, and sometimes they are successful. This is often true when there is a patent behind the product, or when a product becomes more valuable as more people use it, such as social media. But in most cases the chances of success are not higher if you move first. And when the market is not clear, or unknown, then being a pioneer is a huge risk. The lesson here is that, if you have an original idea, it's a mistake to think you must move first, before your competitors. Procrastinating can make it easier to achieve something, and, in the same way, delaying market entry can give us the chance to learn more and reduce risk.

But what happens if we take a wider view than ideas and products? If we look at the whole life of a person, is there a risk in waiting too long?

Conceptual and experimental

It is widely believed that originality is something we find in young people. Vinod Khosla said at the National Association of Software and Services Companies Product Conclave in 2011: "People under thirty-five are the people who make change happen. People over forty-five die in terms of new ideas." Albert Einstein also said that a scientist had to make his discoveries before the age of thirty. And it is true that people do often lose their originality over time.

But this doesn't always happen. When companies have suggestion boxes, it seems that older employees have more and better ideas than younger employees, with the highest-value ideas coming from employees over fifty-five. And in new technology companies, the average age of entrepreneurs is thirty-eight.

In art and science, David Galenson shows that we're quick to remember the exciting young people, but there are a lot of older people who succeed much later. In film, for example, Orson Welles made *Citizen Kane* when he was twenty-five; Alfred Hitchcock made his three greatest films when he was much older, at ages fifty-nine (*Vertigo*), sixty (*North by Northwest*), and sixty-one (*Psycho*). Why are some people creative early, while others start to be creative later?

The creative age depends on the way we think. When Galenson studied creativity he discovered two very different types of thinking: conceptual and experimental. Conceptual people think of a big idea and try to achieve it. Experimental people work by trying different things, some of which succeed, while some don't. They are thinking about a problem, but they don't think about the answer to the problem when they start work. They don't plan; they decide things as they work.

Galenson believes conceptual thinkers move quickly, while experimental thinkers take longer. He studied economists who had won the Nobel Prize and discovered that on average the conceptual economists had done their best work at forty-three, while the experimental economists had done theirs at sixty-one.

A study of physicists who had won the Nobel Prize discovered that half of those under thirty were conceptual, while 92% of those over forty-five did experimental work.

Conceptual people can work quickly because they don't need to do years of careful research. They are also usually young, because young people find it easier to approach a problem in a new way. But as they get older they find it more difficult, and they become less original.

This was Einstein's problem. His most important discoveries were made in his head. They were ideas that explained things that had been discovered by experimental scientists. As he got older, he found it more difficult to work with some of the newer ideas in physics.

Conceptual people have ideas earlier, but then they risk copying themselves and producing very similar ideas. Being experimental takes longer, but it means the scientist or artist is able to discover new ideas. Mark Twain published *Adventures of Huckleberry Finn* when he was forty-nine, changing the story as he wrote it. When he started, he didn't know how it was going to end.

As we get older, it helps to be more experimental. Leonardo da Vinci was experimental, taking years to finish his greatest paintings. Martin Luther King, Jr., too, was experimental, giving thousands of speeches and changing them as he did so. Moving quickly is fine for the young, and creativity can be both conceptual and experimental. But slow and thoughtful can often work better for the older person.

CHAPTER FIVE

How to build coalitions

Many people have forgotten her, but no one did more for women's **suffrage** in America than Lucy Stone. She was the first woman in America to keep her own name after getting married. She was the first woman in Massachusetts to earn a college degree. She was the first American lecturer in women's **rights**. She was one of only a very few women who spoke in public at all. She started the country's leading women's newspaper, the *Woman's Journal*, which was published for fifty years.

In 1851, Stone organized a women's rights meeting, but she wasn't persuaded to speak until the last day. In her speech, she suggested that women should ask the government for the right to vote and to own houses and land. Her speech became known for pushing the women's rights movement forward. Her words were read by John Stuart Mill and Harriet Taylor Mill in England, who later published a famous letter about women's rights.

After the speech, two other great women, Susan B. Anthony and Elizabeth Cady Stanton, joined Stone, and together they worked for women's suffrage. But a long time before they reached their goal the three women broke apart. In 1869, Anthony and Stanton left Stone's organization and started their own. Working separately, the two organizations had little success, and the arguments between the three women made many people think women weren't able to be leaders. When Stanton and Anthony wrote a book about the history of the women's rights movement,

Stone's name wasn't mentioned. If all three leaders wanted the same thing, why did they fight so bitterly?

This chapter looks at how originals build coalitions to reach their goals and how to solve the problems that can lead to coalitions failing. Coalitions can do a lot, but they can also break apart easily because they depend on people's relationships. We will look at the difficulties of coalitions, at an entrepreneur's battle to persuade people to try her idea, at a Disney movie that almost didn't get made, and at how **Occupy** Wall Street failed. You will see how building good coalitions requires a lot of work.

The important lesson is the "Goldilocks" theory of coalitions, which looks at the ideas within groups as too hot, too cold, or just right. The originals who start a coalition are often the most enthusiastic people in it, and sometimes their ideas are too hot for others. It's sometimes necessary to cool the message to encourage other groups to join the coalition. The message needs to be neither too hot, nor too cold. It needs to be just right.

Groups that break

We would expect that having similar goals holds groups together, but very often these goals drive groups apart. Even though people share the same goals, some groups push their ideas further, and these groups are often very **critical** of those who are less enthusiastic. In one study, vegetarians (who don't eat meat) and vegans (who don't eat meat or any other animal products like milk or eggs) gave their opinions about one another. Vegans disliked vegetarians three times as much as vegetarians disliked vegans. The vegans with the strongest opinions thought that vegetarians were weak: if they really cared about animals, they wouldn't eat animal products like eggs. The more strongly you feel about something, the more you want to show you are different from people who have some of your goals but who don't push their ideas as far as you do.

This is why Anthony and Stanton broke away from Lucy Stone. They wanted to push things further. Things got really bad when Anthony and Stanton argued against giving African-American men the vote. If women couldn't vote, they said, these men shouldn't be able to vote either. Stone did not agree; she wanted suffrage for African Americans. Anthony and Stanton were very angry; they thought Stone was not serious about women's suffrage, and they started their own women's suffrage organization. Stone tried to calm things down, but for twenty years their two groups worked separately, sometimes even against one another.

Now there were two separate groups, they needed to find new people to help them and form new coalitions. They all found help from an unexpected group, the Women's Christian Temperance Union, a women's group that was trying to stop people drinking alcohol. Men who drank alcohol were often violent with their wives, and their families became poor. But the WCTU members were very different from the women's suffrage groups. They were often women from rich, usually very religious, families who did not support modern ideas. Yet the groups managed to work together. Many people across the country disliked the idea of women's suffrage, and it's a surprise that the WCTU was happy to work with groups who were pushing for it. But they did make progress, and, in several states, women achieved the right to vote.

The following example of a young, creative entrepreneur shows how business coalitions can be built successfully.

Building and breaking coalitions

In 2011, a student called Meredith Perry realized that there was a big problem with the world of technology. She didn't need a **wire** to make a phone call or connect to the internet. Everything was wireless. Except for one thing. To use her phone and her computer she still had to connect them to the wall to **charge** them. She wanted wireless electricity.

She thought about things that can send energy through the air, like radio **waves**. But they wouldn't work well for electricity. What about **ultrasound**? You can't see ultrasound, and it is silent. Could it be used to carry electrical energy without wires?

Her physics teachers said it was impossible; so did ultrasound engineers. A lot of important people told her she was wasting her time. Then she won an invention competition. But as an entrepreneur on her own, with no money, she needed help.

Three years later, I met Meredith Perry. She had managed to get $750,000 from investors, and she had the first example of a wireless charger. It could charge things faster than a wire, and over longer distances, and it would be in the stores in two years. By the end of 2014, her company, uBeam, had eighteen patents, and investors had given it $10 million. "Every single person that is now working for the company didn't think it was possible," she said.

Perry had had the same difficulty that all originals have when they want to do something different. Most people don't want to change things. She had talked to a lot of experts, and they all told her about the problems in her math and her physics. In the end, she realized there was a problem with her message. She had been saying: "I'm trying to build something that can send electricity through the air." Instead, she said: "I'm looking for someone to make a part for this new product. Can you help?"

This worked. By breaking up the project into parts, she found people who would design those parts. Soon she had people working on the project. She stopped talking about the most exciting part of her idea, the wireless electricity, because that shocked people. She had moved her question from why, to how. Instead of talking about why she wanted something, she talked about how she needed to get there. By talking about smaller parts of the project she found people who would work with her. When she couldn't find engineers to make a big jump, she found engineers who would take a few small steps.

Although it's usually a good idea for creative people to explain why they want to do something, if their idea moves too far from what people think is possible, it may just frighten them away.

Coalitions often break up when one group is more **extreme** than the other groups. Occupy Wall Street started in 2011, to argue against the unequal sharing of money across the United States by the financial center of Wall Street in New York. In 2011, most Americans supported the coalition, but support started to fall as some groups in the coalition became too extreme. Srđa Popović has suggested that the movement's mistake was to use the word "Occupy" in their name, which was about people camping in the streets outside of banks and financial businesses. Although many people approved of the general goals of the movement, they didn't like the idea of "occupying" a place, because it was too extreme.

In the women's suffrage movement something similar happened. Anthony and Stanton built a coalition with George Francis Train in 1867. Train was popular, but he was strongly against giving African-American men the right to vote. It was a dangerous coalition that didn't work. The state of Kansas was close to approving women's suffrage but failed. And African-American men didn't get the right to vote in Kansas either.

Later, Anthony and Stanton put together a coalition with Victoria Woodhull, who was a woman with very strong views and believed that women should have the right to love who they wanted, and, as she said, "to change that love every day if I please." This was too much for many people and frightened away some of the supporters of women's suffrage. Many people think that this delayed women's suffrage for twenty years.

A recent study by Blake Ashforth and Peter Reingen shows an interesting thing about coalitions. For people *inside* a coalition, the most important people are the people at the center of the group. For the women's suffrage coalition, this was Anthony and Stanton. But for people *outside* of a coalition, the person they notice is the one with the most extreme ideas. In the women's suffrage coalition, that person was Woodhull.

Enemies are better than frenemies

In *The Godfather: Part II*, Michael Corleone says, "Keep your friends close, but your enemies closer." But what do we do with people who are neither our friends, nor our enemies?

Usually we see people as friends, enemies, or as somewhere in between. Our closest friends support us all the time; our enemies are always working against us. But in fact there are also people who we can call "frenemies." These are people who sometimes support you and sometimes work against you.

Michelle Duffy, a professor at the University of Minnesota, did a study of police officers and how they felt supported, or not, by the officer that they worked with. Not surprisingly, negative relationships led to stress. When officers felt they weren't supported by the officer they worked with, they didn't work so hard and took more time off of work.

But what happened when the police officer felt supported by the other officer for some of the time? Things didn't get better; they got worse. Negative relationships aren't good, but at least you know what is going to happen, and you can be ready for it. But when you don't know whether someone will support you or not, your stress increases. In another study, Bert Uchino found that "frenemy" relationships like this were unhealthier than bad relationships. People with a lot of relationships that were neither friends nor enemies had higher stress, were unhappier, and found life more difficult than other people.

We may feel it is better to keep away from our enemies and to try to improve our relationship with frenemies. But that is probably not the best idea. It's better to keep away from frenemies and try to turn enemies into friends. Very often the best supporters we have are people who didn't support us in the past, but who have now come over to our side.

First, when someone has always supported us, we expect it and don't think it is that wonderful. But, when someone who didn't support us starts to become a friend, we like them even more. Second, they will feel the same about us. They've worked hard to beat their negative feelings about us, and now they feel much more positively toward us.

Third, and most important, our old enemies are the best at persuading other people to join our movement. They felt negatively about our ideas before, so they understand the people who still feel negatively. And they know why they changed their minds, so they can explain this to others. People will listen to them because they know they weren't always our friends.

When Lucy Stone, who was working for both women's suffrage and African-American suffrage, walked around towns putting up posters for meetings, young men often followed her, pulling the posters down. Stone asked them if they loved their mothers. Of course. Did they love their sisters? Certainly. She then explained that in the south of the United States, African-American men of their age were sold and would never see their families again. She then invited the young men to her meetings as her special guests. Some of these men helped her, and they were very useful when other young men started to make trouble.

From unknown to known

In the 1990s, a group of writers suggested something that had never been done at Disney. Instead of the old stories like *Cinderella* and *Snow White*, they wanted to write something completely new. Nobody at Disney really thought it was a good idea.

The story became *The Lion King*, the most successful film of 1994, winning two Oscars and a Golden Globe. Disney hoped the film would make $50 million. By 2014, it had made more than $1 billion.

Early in the project, five of the writers had a meeting with Disney management, where they explained their story about lions. Michael Eisner, Disney **CEO (Chief Executive Officer)**, tried to find something he could understand in it. "Could you make this into Shakespeare's *King Lear*?" he asked.

That wasn't really possible. But then, from the back of the room, Maureen Donley said, "No, this is *Hamlet*." Suddenly, everyone understood. The uncle kills the father, and then the son has to kill his uncle. So the film became *Hamlet* with lions, and Disney decided to make it.

Justin Berg, a professor at Stanford University, has explained that the writers had to start with the lions. If they had started with *Hamlet*, the story would have been too much like Shakespeare's. Beginning in a different place, with lions, made the story more original, but it provided other difficulties. With a completely original story, people very easily get lost. After starting with the original lions, the writers found that *Hamlet* could help them a lot. For example, they realized that they needed Simba to think about his future, as Hamlet does in his "to be or not to be" speech, so they wrote a new conversation in the film, where Rafiki tells Simba that he must remember where he comes from.

Creating coalitions

Frances Willard became leader of the WCTU after the group began working with the women's suffrage groups. How could she link women's suffrage to the problems of alcohol, which were the WCTU's first interest?

Willard didn't talk about suffrage, but about home protection. The idea of home protection was central to many women, especially religious women. Willard used religion a lot in her speeches, and the WCTU supporters liked that. But she also explained that women's suffrage was the best way of protecting women from men drinking alcohol and being violent.

To return to the Goldilocks idea again, the idea of women having the right to vote was "too hot" for some people. The idea of home protection was "too cold" for others. But, when women's leaders explained how women could make things better for everybody, things were neither too hot nor too cold, and soon women achieved the right to vote in a number of states.

After twenty years of fighting, the two women's suffrage organizations wanted to work together again. But it was very difficult for Stone to work with Anthony; they had been fighting for years, and the relationship was broken. After three years, in 1890, Stone realized it was impossible. She asked her daughter and her daughter's husband to take on the job, and the two organizations did come together.

When Lucy Stone was dying, in 1893, she whispered to her daughter: "Make the world better." It took another twenty-seven years before women's suffrage was achieved in the United States, in 1920, but Stone had done a lot of the early work toward it.

CHAPTER SIX

How to be a rebel

A few seconds ago, he was standing calmly on third **base**. Now his feet are dancing. He is ready to run to home base.

He has been here before. He is one of the greatest players ever to play baseball. Four times he has led his team to the World Series, and all four times they have lost to the Yankees. Now his team is down 6–4 in the eighth **inning**. Is it time to try to steal home?

Stealing a base is one of the riskiest moves in baseball. It increases your team's chances of scoring by only 3%, and to do it successfully you have to slide into the base at high speed, and there is a good chance you will hurt yourself. Stealing home base is even riskier than stealing other bases, because the **pitcher** can see you and he has an easy throw. The pitcher has to throw the ball 60 feet; you have to run 90 feet, so you have to run faster than the ball. And your chances of getting hurt when you are running to home base are four times higher. In the whole of the 2012 season, only three players tried to steal home.

This man, though, is different. He has stolen home base more than any other player of the day—nineteen times. In 100 years only two other players have managed more than nine. But if you think stealing base is about speed, think again. He's thirty-six now, no longer a young man. He's been injured for part of the season. Six years ago he stole thirty-seven bases in a season, but he has stolen far fewer in the last two seasons. His hair is silver, and he weighs more than he used to. This will be his last season.

But this man has spent his life taking action when others stood and watched, and he's not going to stop now. He waits for the right time and then runs. He slides into home base just in time.

It's too little, too late. His team loses the first game to the Yankees. But the effect on the team is enormous. They are on fire for the rest of the season and go on to win.

Years later, a journalist said that this man's attempts to steal home base were the second-bravest thing he had ever done.

The first was becoming Major League Baseball's first black player, in 1947.

To become original we need to take some risks. We can never be sure that we will succeed. As journalist Robert Quillen wrote in 1924, "Progress always involves risk. You can't steal second and keep one foot on first base."

From the start, Jackie Robinson had to deal with white players who refused to play with or against him, as well as hate mail. What made him so brave? We can begin to find the answer by looking at the families of players who are good at stealing bases. Since 1962, only ten players have stolen at least seventy bases in two different seasons. Do you see anything interesting here? Look at the table on the next page.

Trying to find out why some baseball players steal more bases than other players, Frank Sulloway and Richard Zweigenhaft found more than 400 men who played professional baseball. Then they found something surprising. Birth **order** can tell you which man will try to steal most bases. Younger brothers were 10.6 times more likely than older brothers to try to steal.

Baseball player	Steals	Birthplace	Birth Order	Children in Family
Rickey Henderson	130, 108	Chicago, Illinois	4	7
Lou Brock	118, 74	El Dorado, Arkansas	7	9
Vince Coleman	110, 109	Jacksonville, Florida	1	1
Maury Wills	104, 94	Washington, D.C.	7	13
Ron LeFlore	97, 78	Detroit, Michigan	3	4
Omar Moreno	96, 77	Puerto Armuelles, Panama	8	10
Tim Raines	90, 78	Sanford, Florida	5	7
Willie Wilson	83, 79	Montgomery, Alabama	1	1
Marquis Grissom	78, 76	Atlanta, Georgia	14	15
Kenny Lofton	75, 70	East Chicago, Indiana	1	1

Younger brothers weren't better players in other ways. The big difference was in how often they took risks. And they didn't just take more risks; they were 3.2 times more likely to steal a base safely.

The desire to take risks actually means that younger brothers are less likely to play baseball. Across twenty-four studies of more than 8,000 people, younger brothers and sisters were 1.48 times more likely to choose sports where there are more injuries, such as football, rugby, diving, skiing, and car racing. Older brothers and sisters preferred safer sports: baseball, golf, tennis, rowing, and cycling.

If we look at the three players who have stolen the most bases, Jackie Robinson was the youngest of five children. Rod Carew, who comes second in the number of steals, is fourth of five children. And third is Paul Molitor, who is the fourth child of eight.

Younger children are not just risk-takers in baseball. There are differences in politics and science, too. Sulloway researched nearly 4,000 scientists to see what they had said when revolutionary ideas appeared. He looked at the ideas of major scientists such as Copernicus, Darwin, Newton, and Einstein, and he researched what 4,000 other scientists had written at the time. Had they supported these revolutionary ideas or not?

Compared to firstborn children, scientists who were younger children were three times more likely to support Newton and Einstein at the time when their theories were revolutionary. In the fifty years after Copernicus published his idea that the earth went around the sun, scientists who were younger children were 5.4 times more likely to support Copernicus' ideas than firstborn scientists.

We often expect that younger scientists are more likely to support new ideas. But Sulloway shows that birth order is actually more important than age.

As a firstborn myself, I was a little upset by this research. But, as I learned more, I realized that the effects of birth order can be avoided. By bringing up all children in a similar way to younger children, we can raise any child to be more original.

This chapter looks at how the family affects originality. What is special about being a younger child, does family size matter, and how can this affect the way we raise our children? I'll use birth order as a way of looking at the effect family has on how likely we are to take risks. To see how brothers and sisters are more different than we expect, we'll look at how Jackie Robinson was raised, and also at the early years of some of the greatest comedy stars in America. You'll also find out how parents congratulate children in the wrong way and how reading stories can help originality.

Born to be a rebel

One day in 1944, when he was still in the army, Jackie Robinson refused to sit at the back of a bus with other African Americans. The driver "shouted that if I didn't move to the [back] of the bus he would cause me plenty of trouble," Robinson remembered. Robinson told the driver he couldn't care less about the driver causing him trouble. When Robinson talked about his attempt to steal home base in the World Series, he used similar language. "I just took off and did it. I really didn't care whether I made it or not."

"I really didn't care" tells us something important about Jackie Robinson and what he had learned about risk. Many people, when they are deciding what to do, think about how to get the best results. But someone like Robinson thinks differently. What is the right thing for someone like *me* to do? These people don't look at other people. They decide by looking at themselves. The first group of people, who think about the results and what other people will think, can always find a reason not to take a risk. And this sort of decision can be decided by birth order.

For many years, experts have argued that it is helpful to be firstborn. When he or she is born, the first child doesn't have to share parents with brothers or sisters and gets a lot more of their parents' time. Firstborns are more likely to win a Nobel Prize for science, or to get into the United States Congress. Research into 1,500 CEOs shows that 43% of them were firstborn.

In Europe, it was shown that firstborns earn salaries that are 14% higher than their younger brothers and sisters when they start work. But the situation changes by the time they reach the age of thirty. The salaries of those born later grow faster because they are willing to change jobs sooner and more often. Firstborns avoid risk more than those born after them. Those born later are more likely to drink or smoke, and they are less likely to have good insurance.

Although many people now think that birth order has some effect, the science of birth order has many critics. Birth order doesn't fix you in any way, it only affects the direction in which you will probably develop. There are a lot of other things that can affect you. It's difficult for research to look at birth order on its own; there are too many other things that can affect development. But when I looked at birth order I discovered that it was a better way of deciding whether a person would be a risk-taker than I had expected.

In one study, people scored their brothers and sisters and themselves on school achievement and on whether they were **rebels** or not. A rebel is someone who doesn't accept the default. People with high school achievement were 2.3 times more likely to be born first than last. Rebels were twice as likely to be born last than first. There are two possible ways to explain the risk-taking in those born later. One is about how children deal with arguments with their brothers and sisters. The other is about how parents raise younger children differently. Although we can't control birth order, we can change some of its effects.

Niche picking

Look at a lot of brothers and sisters and you will see the big differences in **personality** aren't between families, but between children in families. As adults, brothers and sisters from the same family are different in how much risk they want to take, or how much they rebel, even though they have been raised by the same parents.

Niche picking may help to explain this. The idea was developed by Alfred Adler, who thought that Sigmund Freud's theories about parents didn't explain the part that brothers and sisters play in the development of one another's personality. Adler suggested that because firstborn children start life as only children they learn from their parents. When second or third children come along, the first child risks losing its first place, so may decide to take on the job of being a parent and give orders to the younger child. The younger child answers this by becoming a rebel.

It can be difficult to compete with an older brother or sister, so the younger child has to choose a different path. The niche of the responsible academic achiever is often taken by the first child. Once the first child has taken this niche, it can be difficult for the next to compete. This depends on the age difference; if it's only one year, the younger child may be able to compete. And if it's seven years, the niche may be open again. In baseball, brothers who were between two and five years apart were more likely to play in different positions than brothers who were less than two or more than five years apart. Jackie Robinson was a runner at college, but he couldn't compete with his older brother

Mack, who was five years older and won a silver medal at the 1936 Olympic Games. Jackie Robinson changed to basketball, football, and then baseball.

Outside of the world of sports, I decided to look at comedy. Comedy seems like a risky job, so we would expect younger children to be more successful. I looked at a 2004 list of the 100 greatest comedy performers. You would expect an equal number of any group of 100 to be born first, or born last. However, when I looked at these 100 people, forty-four of them were born last, while only twenty were born first. They came from families with an average of 3.5 children, but nearly half were the baby of their families.

When I looked at particular performers, I found that their older brothers and sisters were often responsible achievers. For example, Chelsea Handler's five older brothers and sisters are an engineer, a chef, an accountant, a lawyer, and a nurse.

Niche picking shows how younger children often try to be different from their older brothers and sisters. Parents may try to give each child the same experience, but birth order pushes their personalities in different directions.

Less responsibility

If Jackie Robinson had been a first child, he would have been raised mainly by his mother. But, with five children to feed, Mrs. Robinson needed to work. Robinson's older sister, Willa Mae, washed him, dressed him, and fed him. And when she went to school, she took her baby brother with her, and he played outside of the classroom. And, if he got into fights, his older brother Frank was there to defend him. When older brothers and sisters behave like parents, there aren't as many rules or punishments, and younger children take risks earlier.

Parents often become more relaxed with the younger children, and things are not so strict. And as the older children take on more responsibilities, there is less need for the younger child to be responsible. The larger the family, the more the younger children can escape responsibility.

We can explain the risk-taking of many originals by their position in the family and the fact that this gives them more freedom and allows them to be rebels. But parents can encourage children to be original whether they are the first or the last. But one of the dangers of originality is that being a rebel is not always positive; it can also be negative. Some research into how parents deal with good or bad behavior will be helpful here.

Explaining and correcting

Some years ago, researchers found that, between the ages of two and ten, parents ask their children to change their behavior once every six to nine minutes. This means perhaps fifty times a day, or more than 15,000 times a year.

For their Altruistic Personality Study, Samuel and Pearl Oliner studied people who had taken great risks to save **Jews** during the Holocaust between 1940 and 1945, when 6 million Jews were murdered. They discovered there was a difference in how parents had corrected the mistakes of those risk-takers when they were children. Their parents explained *why* they were correcting them 21% of the time, compared to 6% of the time for other parents. One interviewee said that her mother "told me when I did something wrong . . . She tried to make me understand with my mind what I'd done wrong." The Oliners also found that explaining was especially useful when it made children think what would happen to other people as a result of their actions.

This can also work with adults. In hospitals, to encourage doctors and nurses to wash their hands more often, David Hofmann and I put two different signs next to soap machines.

Washing your hands stops you catching illnesses.	**Washing your hands stops patients catching illnesses.**

Over the next two weeks we counted the number of times doctors and nurses washed their hands, before and after seeing a patient. The sign on the left made no difference. But the sign on the right made a big difference: using the word "patients" instead of "you" resulted in 10% more hand washing and 45% more soap being used. Thinking about other people changed doctors' and nurses' behavior more than thinking about themselves.

Behavior and character

Good behavior is encouraged partly by what parents say after a child has done the right thing. The last time you saw a child doing something good, you probably talked about what they had done. "That was so sweet." By talking about their behavior you encourage them to do it again. But Joan Grusec did an interesting experiment about this. After some children shared toys with other children, some of them had their behavior mentioned in feedback: "It was nice of you to share those toys with other children. That was a nice and helpful thing to do." Others were given feedback on their characters: "I guess you are the kind of person who likes to help others. You are a helpful person."

Later, in a similar situation, the children who had received character comments were 45% more likely to share toys, while those who received behavior comments were only 10% more likely to share. When our character is mentioned we begin to build up an idea of ourselves as a good person.

It has been suggested that the message "Don't drink and drive" might be better if it were changed to "Don't be a drunk driver." The same idea can be used for originality. When a child produces a good painting, rather than saying that their work is creative we could say "*You* are creative." When we move from talking about behavior to talking about character, people think differently.

Why parents aren't the best role models

We can give children quite a lot of freedom if we explain how what they do affects other people. They will be more likely to be original in a positive way, rather than a negative one. But, as they grow up, they often don't aim high enough.

Parents can begin the development of originality in their children, but as children get older they need **role models**— people who have been original in their own area of work. Jackie Robinson, for example, found a role model in a young mechanic. As a boy, there was a danger that Robinson would become a member of a criminal gang, but this mechanic explained to

Robinson that he was hurting his mother. Martin Luther King, Jr. had Gandhi as a role model, as did Nelson Mandela.

Some originals have found role models in fiction. For example, Sheryl Sandberg and Jeff Bezos have both mentioned finding a role model in the book *A Wrinkle in Time*, in which a young girl learns to bend the laws of physics and travel through time. There are studies that show that, when children's stories show original achievements, people **innovate** more twenty to forty years later. In one study, psychologists noted that original achievement increased in American children's books by 66% between 1810 and 1850. Between 1850 and 1890, the number of patents increased by 700%. Children's books reflected popular values at the time but also helped to create values. It takes time for children to learn originality from characters in fiction. We can be sure that the next group of originals will have been affected by Harry Potter, books where there is a lot of original achievement.

When children read about heroes who are also originals, it may change the way they pick their niches in the family. Wherever we are in family birth order there are niches for us, and role models for originality.

CHAPTER SEVEN

Groupthink

Standing on stage in front of his audience, a technology inventor pulled something out of his pocket. It was so much smaller than competing products that nobody in the room could believe it. He was a man known for his originality and creativity, and he didn't believe in market research. He said his company makes products that people do not even know they want. This man made his company great, only to be forced out, and then watch his company disappear.

The story seems to describe Steve Jobs, but actually this man was one of Jobs' heroes: Edwin Land, the man behind Polaroid. Today, Land is remembered for inventing the **instant** camera. But Land also invented something much more important: the light **filter** that is used in billions of products, from sunglasses to watches. Land was responsible for 535 patents, more than any American before him except for Thomas Edison.

Land was certainly a great original, but his company did not encourage originality. Polaroid was one of the companies that started work on the digital camera, but in the end the company failed because of it. Polaroid's engineers had a high-quality digital camera ready in 1992, but the inventors couldn't persuade the company to start selling it until 1996. By then, there were more than forty other digital cameras on the market.

Polaroid made a basic mistake. Within the company, many people thought that customers would always want to have printed pictures, and the important people in the organization didn't question this idea. It was a case of groupthink—the desire to reach agreement instead of allowing disagreement. Groupthink is the enemy of originality.

In a famous study, the psychologist Irving Janis argued that many bad decisions made by the United States government were caused by groupthink. Janis believed that groupthink occurred when people felt they were deeply involved in a group and they wanted to agree with the group, instead of suggesting different ideas. He said that it was the safe, friendly feelings inside a close group that created groupthink.

People accepted Janis' theory for a long time, but it isn't true. Janis did his work in 1973, but researchers now have seen a lot more government documents, and it's clear that these bad decisions were not made by one small, close group. And there was another problem with Janis' theory. Most of the time he looked at groups making bad decisions. But how do we know that it was actually the closeness of the group that caused the bad decisions? Janis needed to compare good and bad decisions to see whether close groups are more likely to make decisions through groupthink.

The theory of close groups causing groupthink isn't true in business either. When researchers looked at successful and failed decisions in management teams at seven major companies, they discovered that close groups weren't more likely to want to agree with each other and refuse different ideas. In fact, close groups often made better business decisions. The same was true in politics.

In this chapter I want to look at what really causes groupthink and what we can do to prevent it. Why do some close groups make bad decisions while others make good ones? I want to see how to fight groupthink and allow original opinions. I'll look at Polaroid's mistakes, and I'll also examine an organization that has an interesting new way of avoiding conformity. You'll see why people often don't listen to original ideas, and why it's sometimes better to ask people to complain about problems rather than to solve them. In the end you'll see what ordinary people and organizations can do to allow originality to develop.

Commitment to organizations

In the 1990s, a group of experts led by James Baron interviewed 200 people who had started technology companies in Silicon Valley. They asked these leaders what sort of organization they were trying to develop when they started out.

They found three major organizational plans: professional, star, and **commitment**. In a professional organization, managers tried to hire people with the right skills—engineers who could write in JavaScript or C++, for example. In a star organization, managers were not so interested in skills as in the future; they looked for the brightest people and didn't worry so much about their skills, because these people would learn quickly.

In a commitment organization, employees were hired to fit company culture. Skills and intelligence were useful, but the important thing was that the employee believed in the company. Commitment organizations wanted to build strong emotional links between employees and to the organization. They often used words like *family* and *love* when they talked about the company.

71

Baron's team wanted to see which type of organization led to the most success. They followed the 200 companies through the 1990s, into the 2000s. They discovered that one organizational culture was much better than the others: commitment.

Where a company had a commitment culture, the number of failures was zero. Not one of them went out of business. But the number of failures for star organizations was high, and professional companies did even worse.

We can see that a commitment culture worked well in the early days of Polaroid when everybody worked hard and there was a desire for originality and quality. When Edwin Land was developing his instant camera, he once worked for eighteen days without stopping, not even changing his clothes. While his competitor, Kodak, hired scientists, Land looked for a mixed group of employees, including women with artistic experience. Just like the commitment organizations in Silicon Valley, he didn't worry about skills or star qualities. He wanted people who would have original ideas and work hard for the company. His employees developed strong emotional links with the company. When you feel like that, it's hard to imagine working somewhere else.

After the instant camera, Polaroid was responsible for two other important new developments in film technology. The first was the use of sepia, or brown, photos. Black-and-white instant photos often faded, and sepia worked better. The person who discovered that was Meroë Morse, who had been a student of art history and had not studied either physics or chemistry in college. She worked so hard that her laboratory worked twenty-four hours a day. The second new product was instant color photography. Howard Rogers, who had been a car mechanic, worked for fifteen years to solve that problem.

Problems with growth

Commitment cultures are very useful at the beginning of the life of an organization, but, over time, things don't usually go so well. Although these companies grow well at first, growth slows down after a time. When employees share a commitment to the company's clear goals, they can work well in a business situation that they understand. But if things keep changing, as they do in the computer or airline industries, the positive things about this strong culture disappear. When the market is changing, these companies find it difficult to look outside of themselves, and they fail to learn and change.

This is what happened with Polaroid. After Land invented the instant camera in 1948, the company went from making under $7 million in 1950 to making $950 million in 1976. During this time, there were no big changes in the industry; customers loved high-quality cameras that printed instant pictures. But, with the development of digital technology, the market began to change, and Polaroid's culture didn't allow the company to move as fast as market developments.

In 1980, Land was contacted by Akio Morita of Sony who suggested that film was not the future and wanted Sony and Polaroid to work together on an electronic camera. Land wasn't interested. He thought only about the chemistry and physics in photography and didn't believe digital photos would ever be good enough. As Polaroid began to have difficulties, Land didn't look outside of his organization. Instead he worked only with his supporters inside the company. He wanted to make an instant movie camera, and he wouldn't listen to any critics. When it was ready it wasn't a success. It made only a few minutes of video, while competitors already had cameras that could make several hours. The company lost $600 million, and Land lost his job.

Land was not alone in the way he behaved. Research shows that the worse a company does, the more the bosses get advice only from the people who agree with them. But this is the opposite of what they should do; different opinions are useful even when they are wrong.

The evidence suggests that it isn't social links that create groupthink, but too much confidence. Polaroid had too much confidence that customers would always want printed pictures, and they refused to look at other original ideas. So how can you build a strong culture that welcomes disagreement?

Think differently
When I asked entrepreneurs and students about the strongest culture they had ever met in an organization, the winner was Bridgewater Associates. This company in Connecticut manages over $170 billion for governments, universities, and other organizations. The company culture is explained in a book of 200 key ideas. Although the company manages money, none of these ideas are about money. They are about how to behave in any situation that you meet at work or outside.

New employees are hired only if they **fit in** with the company's ideas, and there is a camp where they study and discuss them. Although there is a lot of discussion, Bridgewater is a close, friendly organization. Many employees call it a family, and people often work there for a long time.

Although Bridgewater has a strong commitment culture in an industry that changes all the time, it has continued to be successful for twenty years. Its secret is that it encourages original ideas.

If you are an investor, you can only succeed if you think differently from everyone else. Bridgewater avoids groupthink by inviting different opinions from everyone in the company. When employees share independent ideas instead of agreeing with everyone else, there is a much better chance that Bridgewater will make decisions no one else has thought of. And then there is a better chance they will be right when the rest of the market is wrong.

I want to look now at the culture of the company, which lies behind its brilliant decisions. Bridgewater's success begins with the man who started the company, Ray Dalio. He's been called the Steve Jobs of investing, but employees don't behave as though he is special. They are expected to be critical of him, and employee comments are shared across the company. One of the 200 key ideas is: "No one has the right to hold a critical opinion without speaking up about it." Dalio wants people who think independently and believes that this will make the culture richer and stronger, and better able to avoid groupthink.

Finding complainers

If you're a leader talking to your employees, how would you complete this sentence?

Don't bring me_____; bring me _____.

I learned about this question from David Hofmann, and I've presented it to thousands of groups of leaders. They always shout out the same answer: "Don't bring me problems; bring me answers."

This seems wise. We don't want people just to complain; when they see something wrong, they should find a way to fix it. But when it comes to groupthink this isn't always a good thing. Hofmann has done a lot of research in this area, and he found that a culture that looks mainly at solving problems doesn't encourage people to investigate. If you are expected to always have an answer, you come to meetings ready with your answers, and you don't get the chance to learn from others.

To try to avoid this problem, Google has created a team of "complainers"—engineers across the company who are well-known for recognizing problems and saying what they really think, even if it is negative. Before a major change, managers often ask this team to give critical feedback. By talking to the complainers early, the managers get the feedback, and the complainers often then become the key people to support the change.

Ray Dalio, at Bridgewater, doesn't expect employees to bring him answers. One of the first things he did in the company was to create a list of problems, which any employee could add to. Getting problems noted is half the battle against groupthink;

the other half is listening to the right ideas for solving them. Bridgewater collects a group of people to look at the problems, share their ideas, find out what has gone wrong and why, and suggest ways of solving the problems. It is important that ideas are shared. As Karl Weick advises, "Argue like you're right and listen like you're wrong."

Critical feedback

Even if an organization doesn't encourage critical feedback from its employees, there may be ways of changing the culture. At Index Group, the company CEO, Tom Gerrity, brought in an expert to tell him everything he did wrong in front of his 100 employees. By showing he was happy to get feedback, he found that employees from across the company were more likely to challenge his ideas, and to challenge one another.

I've learned to do something similar in my classroom. I collect feedback from students after the first month, asking for suggestions for improvement. I then email all the feedback to the class. In the next class, I discuss the suggestions, ask for more feedback, and suggest changes. Students often say that this helps them to feel comfortable about becoming more involved in improving the class.

It isn't just the open culture at Bridgewater that makes it easier for employees to challenge managers. When they are new in the company, employees are encouraged to question the company's key ideas. In most companies the employee is busy learning the job for the first few months and isn't encouraged to think about any problems. But in fact those early days, when employees have more time, and before they see the world in the company way, are a good time for them to think about improving the culture.

A few years ago I was hired by Goldman Sachs to help them attract and keep excellent employees by encouraging those employees to improve their place of work. One thing we introduced was an entry interview. Managers have meetings to ask new employees for ideas when they start, instead of waiting to ask employees what they thought of the company when they leave. It's easier to start a relationship with the door open than to try to push open a door that has already been closed.

Movers and shapers

Ray Dalio at Bridgewater is interested in understanding people who shape the world and in finding out how they are similar. He's interviewed many originals of our time and has studied originals from history like Benjamin Franklin and Albert Einstein.

Of course, all of these people were enthusiastic and had great imagination, but Dalio has three other qualities on his list of similarities. First, "shapers" are independent thinkers and rebels who ask a lot of questions. Second, they are honest critics and don't care who they are talking to. And third, they are not afraid of risk; their fear of not succeeding is greater than their fear of failure.

If Dalio doesn't find a shaper to follow him, Bridgewater may go the same way as Polaroid. But Dalio knows that preventing groupthink is about more than the ideas of one leader. The greatest shapers don't stop at introducing originality into the world; they create cultures that encourage originality in others.

CHAPTER EIGHT

Working with emotions

In 2007, a man called Lewis Pugh jumped into the Arctic Sea. The ice was not completely frozen, and Pugh's plan was to be the first person to survive a long-distance swim across the North Pole. Pugh had been in the British Special Air Service before becoming the best cold-water swimmer on the planet. Two years earlier he had jumped off of the ice to swim a kilometer in Antarctica. But he doesn't do it just to be the best in the world; he wants to make people think about climate change.

Before he swims, something happens to Pugh that has never been noticed in any other human; his body temperature goes up from 98.6°F to 101°F. When it is time to get into the freezing water, his body prepares.

The passengers on the *Titanic* died in water that was 41°F. In Pugh's Antarctic swim, the water had been 32°F. At the North Pole, it was less than 29°F. After falling into that water, a British explorer had lost fingers in three minutes; Pugh's team estimated that his swim would take twenty minutes. But a five-minute test swim at the North Pole went badly and, instead of imagining success, Pugh began to imagine failure. If he failed, he would die. He became very afraid and questioned whether he would survive. So would it have been better for him to imagine success?

This chapter looks at the emotional cost of going against the crowd. In my own research in a healthcare company, I tested how much employees knew about how to manage emotions.

Those who showed up well in the emotion test also spoke up more with ideas and suggestions in the workplace, and their managers thought they were better employees. They had the courage to challenge, but they were also able to control their emotions when they were doing it.

To understand these emotional skills, I'll look at how Pugh got ready for the freezing water, and how Martin Luther King, Jr. prepared civil rights workers to keep calm. I'll explore how one group managed to throw out a **dictator**, and how a leader in technology persuaded engineers to make a major change to their product. By studying how to manage emotions, you'll discover whether it's better to plan for success or failure, whether calming yourself down can fight fear, how to deal with your anger, and what it takes to keep going when everything seems to be against you.

Optimism and pessimism

Although many originals seem to be confident on the outside, inside they often worry and doubt their own abilities. When United States government leaders described their most difficult decisions, they didn't talk about difficult problems but about choices that needed courage. And research by Scott Sonenshein has shown that people working for a better environment are often uncertain about whether they can succeed. Challenging the present situation is often hard work, and there will be problems and failures along the way.

Psychologist Julie Norem studies two different ways of managing these challenges: optimism and pessimism. Optimists expect that the best will happen; they stay calm and expect to succeed. Pessimists expect the worst; they worry, and they imagine all the things that can go wrong.

Most people think it's better to be an optimist than a pessimist. Yet Norem found that, although pessimists worry more and are less confident, they do their jobs as well as the optimists. And Norem soon realized that pessimists did well *because* of their pessimism.

Norem explains that pessimism works as a way of managing fear and worry. When pessimists start to doubt themselves, they don't allow themselves to freeze with fear. They imagine an enormous failure to make them worry more, and that gives them reasons to succeed. Once they have imagined everything that can go wrong, they look at how to avoid those problems, and this makes them feel they can control things. They worry most before they act, so when they start to move they are ready to succeed. They are confident because they know they have prepared as well as possible. If they don't worry, then they relax and don't plan. It's important that pessimists don't feel comfortable.

Lewis Pugh was usually an optimist. He took risks when other people would give up. But in the weeks before a major swim he was often more of a pessimist. It was not the words of his own team that encouraged him, but the words of people who doubted him. Two years earlier, before another freezing swim, an expert had told him that it was impossible and that he would die.

As Pugh stood shaking at the North Pole, his pessimism told him that things were not going to go well. But, instead of trying to find reasons to be happier, he started to think about every possible risk. He made plans to be sure that he spent very little time on the ice before the swim and to get to the boat as quickly as possible afterward. "The trick is to make fear your friend," he says on his website (www.lewispugh.com). But this isn't enough. Pessimism can be helpful when you're sure about what you want to do. But, when you're not so sure, doubt can get in the way.

Keep believing

When most people list the things that frighten them, one thing comes up very often: speaking in public. If we want to understand how people manage fear, we can just put them on stage. Alison Wood Brooks asked college students to give a speech about why they would be good to work with. The speeches were filmed, and a group of students was ready to watch them and score them. With only two minutes to prepare, many of the students were actually shaking.

If you were in this situation, how would you manage your fear? When 300 professional workers were asked, 90% suggested "Try to relax and calm down." But this is not the best advice.

Before the college students gave their speeches, Brooks asked them to say three words out loud. Half of them were asked to say "I am calm." The other half were asked to say "I am excited."

Changing one word was enough to change the quality of the speeches. When students attached the label "excited" to their emotions, they were scored as 17% better at persuading and 15% more confident than those students who said they were "calm". The excited students also gave longer speeches than the calm students. In another experiment, when students were nervous before a math test they scored 22% better if they were told "Try to get excited" instead of "Try to remain calm."

Brooks wanted to find out if it's better just to accept worry, so she gave students another frightening task. They were asked to sing in public, and they would be scored on the quality of their singing. This time, one group wasn't asked to say anything before singing, another was asked to say "I am worried," and a third "I am excited." The group who said nothing scored 69%; the group who said "worried" scored only 53%. But the group who said "excited" scored 80%.

When we are frightened, why is it better to make ourselves excited than to try to stay calm? Fear is a strong emotion; when we are frightened, our heart gets faster. If we then try to relax, it's like trying to stop a car suddenly when it's going fast. It's better to take a strong emotion and turn it into something different but equally strong.

Author Susan Cain says that we have a stop system and a go system. When we haven't decided what we are going to do, pessimism is dangerous. Thinking too much about the dangers makes us worry and "stop." Being optimistic makes us more likely to do something—to "go." However, in a situation where we have already decided what we are going to do, and start to worry about it, it is better to be a pessimist and turn our worries into positive emotions like excitement. This switches on our go system.

In previous cold-water swims, Lewis Pugh was certain he would succeed, so being a pessimist was helpful: looking at all the possible dangers made him ready for anything. At the North Pole, this worked at first, but after the five-minute test swim, which went badly, he started to worry: "What I felt on that stupid test swim wasn't like anything I'd felt before. I don't believe I can do this."

It was time to move away from pessimism. A friend gave him three ideas to get excited. First, he reminded Pugh that twenty-nine people from ten countries had helped him, and he put flags from those countries along the water. Second, the friend told him to think of his parents and how they had helped him. And third, he told him to think about climate change and how the swim might help. After listening to his friend, Pugh was ready to do the swim. He jumped into the freezing water and finished, successfully, in eighteen minutes and fifty seconds.

For Pugh, the most difficult thing was managing his own emotions. But other originals have to manage other people's emotions. When others are afraid to act, how can we encourage them?

In 2009, fifteen young tourists visited Belgrade, the capital of Serbia. After walking them around part of the city, their guide, a Serbian in his thirties, talked about the country's recent history of high potato prices and free concerts. But they weren't ordinary tourists, and they were getting impatient. They had come to Belgrade to learn how to get rid of their own country's dictator.

They asked the guide how the people of Serbia had removed the Serbian dictator Slobodan Milošević. You don't need to take big risks, the guide told them. You can do lots of little things —drive more slowly than usual, push televisions through the streets, or turn lights on and off. The tourists just laughed. Small things like that would never work for us, they said. If we did that, we would be arrested and then disappear. How can we have a revolution when we can't meet in groups of more than three?

They didn't know it, but the guide had heard all this before—from Georgians in 2003, from Ukrainians in 2004, from Lebanese in 2005, and from Maldivians in 2008. In each case they had gone back to their countries and removed a dictator. The guide, Srđa Popović, had taught them all. He was one of the people behind Otpor!, the non-violent organization of young people who had helped remove Milošević. Popović had been attacked by the dictator's police and had spent time in jail.

When psychologist Dan McAdams and his team asked adults to tell them their life stories, and how they felt at different times, they saw two patterns. Some people had mostly good experiences and were fairly happy during most of their lives. But people who had found original ways of helping others often had stories that started badly when they were young but got better later. Although they had more bad experiences than the other group, these originals had more happiness. They managed their problems, and in the end their lives were happier and fuller.

After leading the group that removed their dictator, Popović began to help other groups that were trying to remove dictators without violence. Not every group succeeded, but we can learn a lot from Popović's way of managing emotions.

Using users to excite teams

When Josh Silverman took over at Skype in February 2008, the company had problems. Skype, a leader in free computer-to-computer calls, was no longer growing as fast as before. Silverman decided he had to do something big. In April, he announced that Skype 4.0 would appear before the end of the year, and it would include full-screen video. Most employees were deeply negative about this. They thought there wasn't enough time; the video quality would be poor; and users would hate using a full screen.

Silverman didn't try to calm them down but decided he needed to get them excited about video. He talked to employees about the big idea: "It's not about making cheap phone calls. It's about being together when you're not in the same room." Silverman talked about how Skype allowed his children to keep close contact with their grandparents, who were thousands of miles away. Then he let other Skype users talk about what Skype had done for them. A married couple talked about how Skype kept them together when they had to spend a year living apart. A man in the army talked about how he could be with his children even when he was in another country; they even opened Christmas presents together.

As they began to understand that Skype was about connecting people, the team's worries turned to excitement. Their go system was switched on. Skype 4.0 was ready on time with high-quality full-screen video calls. Soon, Skype was adding 380,000 new users every day. Less than three years later, Microsoft bought Skype for $8.5 billion; the company had increased in value by 300%.

In Serbia, Popović knew he had to show people something to encourage them to act. People were too afraid to listen, so Popović used a picture of a **fist** to encourage people's go system.

Strength in numbers

If you are the only person with an idea, it can be hard to defend it. But people can get strength from just a small number of people who think like them. To feel that you're not alone, you don't need a whole crowd. Research by Sigal Barsade and Hakan Ozcelik has shown that, in business or government, even having one friend may be enough.

If you want people to take risks, you have to show them they aren't alone. This was the first part of Otpor!'s success. In 1998, they painted a fist on buildings all around Belgrade, together with sentences like "I am against the government because I love Serbia," "Bite the system," and "Argue until we win." Before they saw the fist, people who were against Milošević were afraid to say what they thought. But, when they saw it, they realized there were others who were happy to take a risk. Later, when police arrested members of Otpor!, those members were often asked who was their leader. Popović and his friends taught them to answer, "I am one of the 20,000 leaders of Otpor!"

Around the world, different organizations have used small actions to show they are part of a larger group. In Chile, to complain about the dictator Pinochet, people turned their lights on and off. When people saw their neighbors doing that, they weren't afraid to do the same. Then people were invited to drive slowly. Taxi drivers slowed down, and so did bus drivers. Soon people were walking slowly in the streets. People understood there was no risk: it's not against the law to drive or walk slowly.

In Poland, when people were unhappy about government news on televisions, they knew that just turning off the television wasn't enough. So they took their televisions outside and pushed them through the streets. It's not against the law to push your television through the streets.

In Serbia, Otpor! found a clever way to change people's fear to excitement: comedy. They sent birthday presents to Milošević: a ticket out of the country, and a prison uniform. It's hard to be afraid of speaking up against a dictator when you are laughing at him.

Laughter can work in other situations where people are afraid, too. When you have no power, laughter is a powerful way to change strong negative emotions into positive ones. After hearing Popović's story, a group of students wanted to do something about the very high cost of lessons at their university. They decided to show the university president pictures of their cheap and simple meals and invite themselves to dinner at his house.

But Popović also has a message that isn't funny at all. At first, Popović seems to be an optimist. When others were ready to give up, he thought there was a better future for Serbia. But when I asked him if he was ever unsure, he told me he had doubts for all of those ten years. Even today, he worries about the people who died, and he feels responsible.

The importance of now

On New Year's Eve in 2000, Popović and his friends organized a celebration in the main square in Belgrade, with music and dancing. At midnight the famous band the Red Hot Chili Peppers would appear, and everyone was very excited. One minute before midnight, the square went dark and people began counting down. But when it was midnight, no famous band appeared. Instead, a voice said, "We have nothing to celebrate. This has been a year of war. But it doesn't have to be that way. Let's make the coming year count. Because 2000 is *the* year."

When John Kotter studied 100 companies that were trying to make major changes, he discovered that the first mistake they made was to fail to make people understand that acting quickly was important. Kotter noted that managers didn't realize how difficult it was to persuade people that change needed to happen, and it needed to happen now. If they don't understand the importance of speed, employees sit back and refuse to change. Otpor! made people in Serbia understand the importance of speed when they announced: "This is *the* year."

To understand this more, let's look at another piece of research by Amos Tversky and Daniel Kahneman. Imagine you are the manager of a car company. Sales are down, and you need to close three factories and lose 6,000 employees. You can choose between two different plans.

Plan A will save one of the three factories and 2,000 jobs.

Plan B has a one-third chance of saving all three factories and 6,000 jobs, but a two-thirds chance of saving no factories and no jobs.

Most people, 80%, prefer Plan A.

But let's now look at the choice in a different way.

Plan A will lose two factories and 4,000 jobs.

Plan B has a two-thirds chance of losing all three factories and 6,000 jobs, but a one-third chance of losing no factories or jobs.

These are the same choices as the first time, but they don't feel like it. In this case, 82% of people prefer Plan B.

In the first case, the choices show what we could gain. We prefer Plan A because it looks less risky. When we are sure we will gain something, we want to keep and protect it. We want to save 2,000 jobs, rather than take a risk and save no jobs. In the second case we are told what we are going to lose. Now we want to avoid losing anything, even if it means taking a bigger risk. We're going to lose thousands of jobs anyway, so we decide to take a big risk and hope that we lose nothing.

If we want people to change, is it better to show them why it is helpful to change, or the costs of not changing? According to Peter Salovey it depends on whether people think the change is safe or risky. If they think it is safe, it is better to talk about the good things that will happen if they do it. They will want to act immediately and get there quickly. But if they think it's risky, that doesn't work. They are comfortable where they are, so they don't see why they should change. If we want them to change, we have to talk about the bad things that will happen if they don't change. It's easier for people to take a risk when they know they will definitely lose something if they don't.

At Merck, the medicine company, they wanted managers to be more involved in making changes. Managers were asked to think of ideas that would put Merck out of business. They imagined that they were one of Merck's competitors and developed ideas for new medicines that were better than Merck's, or looked at markets Merck had missed. Then they had to find ways to defend the company against these competitors.

This "kill the company" exercise is strong because it asks people to think about what they might lose. Before, when managers thought about new products, they didn't want to take risks. But when they thought about their competitors they realized it was a risk *not* to innovate.

Popović realized that strong emotions were needed to change the situation in Serbia. By stopping the concert and sending people home on New Year's Eve, he was reminding them to act now.

Deep and surface acting

Anger is a good way to get people to do something. We feel we have to fight when someone has done the wrong thing. But, although anger can encourage people to speak and to act, it can also make them do it the wrong way. Debra Meyerson and Maureen Scully suggest that the key is to be hot-headed and cool-headed at the same time. The heat pushes us toward action and change; the coolness gives the action a useful shape.

Arlie Hochschild has suggested that if you are feeling a strong emotion like worry or anger there are two ways to manage it: **surface** acting and deep acting. Surface acting means changing your face, speech, and actions to show you are calm. If you are working for an airline and an angry passenger starts to shout at you on a plane, you may smile and try to show some warmth. You change on the outside, but inside you haven't changed. You are angry with the passenger, and the passenger probably knows it. But if you are deep acting you might imagine that the passenger is under stress, is afraid of flying, or has problems at home. You feel sorry for the passenger, and your smile is warmer.

Before Lewis Pugh starts out on one of his swims he uses deep acting. He listens to music and remembers jumping from a plane in his army days. He is returning to the excitement that he felt then, and which he wants to find again. Deep acting is a better way of managing emotions than surface acting. If we want to show our emotions, we have to feel them.

The dangers of venting

Less than a year after Rosa Parks refused to give up her seat on a bus in Montgomery, a United States court decided that separating black and white people was against the law. Now that black people could sit anywhere on a bus, Martin Luther King, Jr. and others realized they needed to help black people reply to the violence that they might meet.

The team put chairs in rows, like a bus, and asked audience members to play "black" or "white" passengers. The "white" passengers called the "black" passengers names, pushed them, and threw things at them. The "black" passengers needed to act deeply. King wanted them to be angry enough to speak out, but not to be so angry that they became violent. What would be the best way to manage their anger? Many people suggest that venting works best, turning the anger against something else like hitting a pillow, or screaming. But studies have shown that venting doesn't help, even if you think it does or it makes you feel good. After venting, most people are even angrier than before.

When King and his team worked on anger, they were careful to stop people venting. Sometimes a person playing a "black" man would get so angry that he hit back. They would work with him so that what he said and did was less violent.

To use anger in a positive way, it is better to avoid thinking too much about the person we are angry with. It is better to think about the people who have been hurt by the person's actions. Martin Luther King, Jr. often did this. He said he was not trying to beat the white man; he wanted to free black children. Thinking about those who have been hurt can lead to a different kind of anger. Research has shown that when we are angry *with* someone we want to hurt them. But when we are angry *for* someone we want to make things better for them. We don't want to punish; we want to help.

When a voice told Serbians there was nothing to celebrate on New Year's Eve, they felt an angry energy. Popović said, "There was an energy in the air that no rock band could ever recreate. Everybody felt that they had something important to do." The next fall Milošević lost the election, and the man who told the people to go home became the president of Serbia four years later.

––––––

E.B. White once wrote that he woke in the morning unable to decide whether he wanted to improve the world or to enjoy the world. He commented in an interview with *The New York Times*, "This makes it difficult to plan the day."

As we search for happiness, many of us choose to enjoy the world as it is. Originals take a more difficult path, trying to make the world what it could be. They may have to forget about their own happiness for a time. Becoming original is not the easiest way to find happiness, but the journey brings its own happiness.

Actions for originality

If you want to encourage originality, here are some actions you can take. The first group of actions is for anyone who wants to develop new ideas. The next group is for leaders. And the final group is for parents and teachers.

Actions for everyone

A. Getting original ideas
1. **Question the default.**
   You don't have to accept the way things are. Remember that the default is decided by people, and it can be changed.
2. **Have three times as many ideas.**
   The best way to originality is to have more ideas.
3. **Learn something new.**
   Start painting or playing the piano, like the Nobel Prize-winning scientists. Or try a different job that needs different skills. Or work in a foreign country, like the fashion designers.
4. **Procrastinate.**
   When you're trying to find new ideas, stop before you have finished, and do something different. You will probably have different and better ideas when you start again.
5. **Get feedback from the people you work with.**
   You can't judge your own ideas well, and managers are often too tough as critics.

B. Making original ideas heard

6. Balance your risks.

If you are going to take a risk in one area, keep other areas of your life safe.

7. Find reasons for not supporting your ideas.

Be like Rufus Griscom. Make a list of the biggest problems with your ideas, and ask others to add to it. Looking at what is wrong can show what is right.

8. Repeat your ideas.

People like ideas more if they have heard them ten to twenty times. It's better if the ideas are short and repeated over a number of days, mixed with other ideas.

9. Speak to a different audience.

Instead of trying to find friendly people who like your ideas, look for difficult people who will be critics of them. Your best supporters are people who are tough and have solved problems like yours.

10. Control the heat.

If your ideas are extreme, and people think they are dangerous, find ways of making them easier for other people to accept. Think about a goal that people already believe in.

C. Managing emotions

11. Think about progress.

When you want to take action, think about the progress you still need to make. You'll find the energy to get there. When you feel less sure, think of the progress you have already made. You can't give up now!

12. **Don't try to calm down.**

If you're nervous, it's hard to relax. Turn your worries into a strong positive emotion like excitement. Think about why you are taking action and how things can be improved.

13. **Think about who has been hurt, *not* who has hurt them.**

Instead of punishing the person who has done wrong, think about the person who has been harmed; it will turn your anger in a positive direction.

14. **Realize you are not alone.**

Having just one person who shares your ideas can be a big help. Find that person, and begin to work together.

15. **If you don't take action, things won't change.**

If you are not happy with something, only walking away or speaking up can help. Speaking up may be best if you have a chance of being listened to. If not, it may be better to leave.

Leader actions

A. Getting original ideas

1. Have a competition for new ideas.

Allowing people to give you ideas any time doesn't help when everybody is busy. Ask for ideas to help with a single problem or need. Give employees three weeks to develop ideas, and then have them judge one another's ideas. The winners get money and people to make the idea really work.

2. **Imagine that you are the enemy.**

   Get people to work quickly by using the "kill the company" idea from Chapter Eight. Ask the group to spend an hour thinking of how to put the company out of business. Then discuss how to defend the company from these dangers.

3. **Ask people from different parts of the company to give you ideas.**

   At DreamWorks Animation, even people in the accounts and law departments are invited to give ideas for movies. This makes work more interesting for employees as well as producing more ideas.

4. **Have an opposite day.**

   Divide people into groups and ask each group to find an idea that most people think is true, or something that most people believe. Then each group asks the question, "When is the opposite true?" and finds ideas to support the opposite.

5. **Don't allow the words "like", "love", and "hate."**

   At the company DoSomething.org, leader Nancy Lublin doesn't allow employees to use the words "like", "love", and "hate." These words make it too easy to give a quick answer without thinking. Instead, employees must explain their thoughts. This encourages people to have new ideas, rather than just rejecting those they don't like.

B. **Building cultures of originality**

6. **Hire people on what they can bring to the company.**

   When leaders hire people because they fit the company culture, they hire people who think the same. Before interviews, think about the kinds of people you need but don't have in your company. Then try to find people like that in the interviews.

7. **Give new employees an entry interview.**

Don't wait until employees leave; ask new employees for ideas when they start working in the company. Ask them why they decided to work for you and what will encourage them to stay.

8. **Ask for problems, not answers.**

Don't ask people to hurry to find answers. As at Bridgewater, keep a list of problems that employees can add to. Meet monthly to look at the problems on the list and decide which problems are really important and need to be solved.

9. **Find people who disagree.**

It's useful to listen to opposite opinions even if they are wrong. Look out for people who can argue against new ideas, and listen to those people.

10. **Invite employees to be critics.**

Encourage employees to be your critics. This will allow employees to speak more openly, and it will allow for better ideas to become available.

Parent and teacher actions

1. **Ask children what their role models would do.**

Children feel freer to act when they look at problems through the eyes of originals. Ask them what they would like to improve at school or at home. Then ask them to find a real or fictional person they admire as an original and to think about what that person would do.

2. **Connect good behavior to good character.**

   Many parents and teachers thank children for their helpful *actions*, but it's better to thank them for being helpful *people*. If you want a child to share a toy, don't ask, "Will you share?", ask, "Will you be a sharer?"

3. **Explain how bad behavior can affect others.**

   When children behave badly, make sure they understand how this harms other people: "How do you think this made her feel?" When children think about how they have hurt others, it can help them avoid that behavior in the future.

4. **Values are important.**

   Encourage children to understand why your values are important to you, and to develop their own values.

5. **Create new niches for your children to explore.**

   Younger children discover new niches when others have been taken by their older brothers and sisters. You can help any child find his or her own niche. One of my classroom favorites is to ask children to work on different parts of a project. For example, when writing about Eleanor Roosevelt's life, one student worked on her early life, one on her years as a teenager, and a third on her time in the women's movement. In this way, each child learned to value other children's strengths and had the space to consider their own ideas instead of being affected by groupthink.

During-reading questions

Write the answers to these questions in your notebook.

CHAPTER ONE

1 What do creative people often not accept?
2 What can hold back creativity?
3 What did an investor in Apple want Steve Wozniak to do?

CHAPTER TWO

1 *Seinfeld* was an example of a false . . .
2 Segway was an example of a false . . .
3 Where have creative fashion designers often worked?

CHAPTER THREE

1 How did Rufus Griscom sell his idea to investors?
2 Why do most people prefer inverted photos of themselves?
3 Why was it especially difficult for Carmen Medina to speak up?
4 Why was it a big risk for Donna Dubinsky when she spoke up?

CHAPTER FOUR

1 When did Martin Luther King, Jr. finish writing his famous speech?
2 What do we call companies that are the first to enter a market?
3 Which employees put the highest-value ideas in company suggestion boxes?

CHAPTER FIVE

1 What did Lucy Stone spend her life working for?
2 What did Meredith Perry want to develop?
3 Why do frenemies lead to more stress than enemies?
4 Why was it helpful to compare *The Lion King* to *Hamlet*?

CHAPTER SIX

1 Jackie Robinson was the first black man to do what?
2 Why does a younger child need to find a different niche?
3 Which usually works better: feedback on behavior or feedback on character?
4 Why are role models important to children as they grow?

CHAPTER SEVEN

1 What did Irving Janis believe caused groupthink?
2 Which three major types of organization culture did James Baron describe?
3 When do companies with a commitment culture meet problems?
4 Which company created a team of "complainers" to get critical feedback?

CHAPTER EIGHT

1 What happens to Lewis Pugh's body temperature before he swims that is so surprising?
2 If you are speaking in public, which three words can you repeat before speaking to improve your speech?
3 What three things did Lewis Pugh think about during his swim?
4 Who was the leader of Otpor!?

After-reading questions

1 Look back at the "Before-reading questions" on page 5. Which people were discussed in the book? Which products were mentioned?

2 What's the best thing to do with defaults?

3 Why is it important for originals to produce a large number of ideas?

4 Why is it a good idea to repeat ideas?

5 How does procrastinating help creativity?

6 Which person in a coalition do people outside of the coalition notice most? How is this different from who people inside the coalition notice most?

7 Why is it a good idea to explain to children how their behavior affects others?

8 What does Adam Grant (the author) believe causes groupthink?

9 When is pessimism helpful? And when is it better to be optimistic?

Exercises

1 **Write the correct words in your notebook.**

1 svetin ....*invest*............ To lend money to a company in the hope of making a profit.

2 nlgoriia .... A person who has and can develop new ideas.

3 oyntmcofri .... Doing the same things as most other people.

4 uftdeal .... The usual way that something is done.

5 tryreuoalionv .... A person who wants to make big, perhaps violent, changes.

6 eereentrrpnu .... A person who starts a business.

7 eydla .... To do something late.

8 rfaleui .... The opposite of success.

2 **Complete the sentences in your notebook, using the words from the box.**

inventions	positive	artistic	negative
	canceled	transportation	

1 Dean Kamen was behind a number of medical ......*inventions*........

2 The television company nearly .... *Seinfeld*.

3 A false .... is something that people expect to succeed, but it doesn't.

4 A false .... is something that people expect to fail, but it doesn't.

5 Nobel Prize winners are more likely to do .... activities than other scientists.

6 The early investors in Segway didn't understand ....

103

3 **Complete these sentences in your notebook, using the verbs from the box.**

could	should	might

1 If Segway had done the same as Warby Parker, they ....*might*.......... have avoided some of their problems.

2 When people without status make suggestions, we don't think they .... tell us what to do.

3 Rufus Griscom advised investors why they .... not invest in *Babble*.

4 You .... have thought that Martin Luther King, Jr. would begin to write his speech immediately.

5 Martin Luther King, Jr. got advice from three people about what he .... say.

6 If Mahalia Jackson hadn't shouted behind him, King .... not have talked about his dream.

7 Martin Luther King, Jr. had a lot of material in his head that he .... use if he wanted to.

8 Kozmo .... have competed with Netflix if they had moved more slowly.

4 Complete these sentences in your notebook, using the words from the box.

> procrastinated   alcohol   wire   extreme
> equality   suffrage   charge   degree

1 Martin Luther King, Jr. didn't write his speech immediately: he ....*procrastinated*..........
2 For Abraham Lincoln, the Civil War was about freedom and ....
3 Lucy Stone was the first woman in Massachusetts to earn a college ....
4 In 2011, Meredith Perry realized that you didn't need a .... to connect to the internet, but you did to charge things.
5 To .... your phone you usually have to connect it to the wall.
6 Coalitions often break up when one group is more .... than the others.
7 One women's group wanted to stop people drinking ....
8 Women worked for many years before they achieved ....

CHAPTER FIVE

5 Write the correct nouns in your notebook. Sometimes the noun and the verb are the same.

1 move ....*movement*........   2 succeed
3 compete   4 invent
5 charge   6 frighten
7 support   8 protect

6 **Complete these sentences in your notebook, using the correct form of the verb.**

1 Since 1962, only ten players ......*have stolen*...... (steal) at least seventy bases in two different seasons.

2 You have to slide into the base at high speed, and there is a good chance you .... (hurt) yourself.

3 Birth order .... (be) actually more important than age.

4 Firstborns .... (avoid) risk more than those born after them.

5 If Jackie Robinson .... (be) a first child, he would have been raised mainly by his mother.

6 Good behavior .... (encourage) partly by what parents say after a child has done the right thing.

7 **Write the correct answers in your notebook.**

1 Edwin Land is remembered as the **invention** / *inventor* of the instant camera.

2 Irving Janis believed that groupthink occurred when people felt they were deeply **involved** / **involving** in a project.

3 In a **committed** / **commitment** organization employees were hired to fit the company culture.

4 When Edwin Land was developing his company, he hired **employees** / **employers** who had original ideas.

5 Bridgewater Associates **invests** / **investigates** money for other organizations.

7 Many organizations encourage **critic** / **critical** feedback from their employees.

8 **Write questions for these answers in your notebook.**

1 Where ....*did Lewis Pugh swim in 2007*........?
   In the Arctic Sea.

2 What ....?
   They expect that the best will happen.

3 What ....?
   They are frightened of speaking in public.

4 How many ....?
   Twenty-nine.

5 What ....?
   He announced that Skype 4.0 would have full-screen video.

6 Who didn't ....?
   The Red Hot Chili Peppers.

7 What ....?
   It means changing your face and actions, but not changing inside.

8 How ....?
   They feel angrier than before.

Project work

1 Choose two original people described in the book, and then a third person who is not in the book but who you feel is also an original. Complete the information listed below in your notebook, and then write 200 words about each person you chose.

- Name
- Dates
- Where they live(d)
- Achievements

2 Choose two original companies described in the book, and then a third company which is not in the book but which you feel has shown originality. Complete the information listed below in your notebook, and then write 200 words about each company you chose.

- Name
- Company start date
- Where the company works/worked
- Type of business
- Original achievements

Essay questions

- Choose one of the chapters between Two and Eight. What are the key ideas in this chapter? How might you change the way you do things to make use of the ideas in the chapter? (500 words)
- Which of the people described in this book do you admire the most? Why is that? (500 words)
- Do you think you are an optimist or a pessimist? Explain why. (500 words)

An answer key for all questions and exercises can be found at **www.penguinreaders.co.uk**

Glossary

achieve (v.)
to succeed in doing something after trying hard

American Declaration of Independence (n.)
an official document from July 4, 1776 that announced that Great Britain would no longer rule thirteen American states

average (n.)
the middle amount or quality of something. If you add two or more numbers together and divide them by the number of numbers that you added, you get the *average*.

base (n.)
one of the four places that a player must run to in a game of baseball

CEO (Chief Executive Officer) (n.)
A *CEO* is the person who has the most important job in a company.

charge (v.)
to put electricity into a machine or battery

CIA (Central Intelligence Agency) (n.)
a part of the United States government that collects secret information about people and organizations

coalition (n.)
two or more groups that have joined together

comedy (n.)
a funny television program, film or play

commitment (n.)
giving your time and energy to something that you believe in

confidence (n.)
knowing that you can do things well

conformity (n.); **conform** (v.)
when you choose to behave in the way that most other people behave because it is expected of you

creativity (n.)
the ability to think of new ideas and produce new things

critical (adj.)
saying that someone or something is wrong or bad

decision (n.)
When you decide something, you make a *decision*.

default (n.)
the way that something is if no changes are made to it

degree (n.)
A university gives a *degree* to a student who has successfully completed a course there.

delay (v.)
to make something happen later than planned or expected

dictator (n.)
a person who leads a country without having an election and who uses the army to rule the people

distribution (n.)
when goods are sent from a place to shops. The place the goods are sent from is called a *distribution* center.

drop out (v.)
If you *drop out* of school or university, you leave there before you have completed your education.

employee (n.)
someone who is paid to work for a company or person

enthusiastic (adj.); **enthusiasm** (n.)
Enthusiasm is the feeling of being interested in or excited about something. If you are *enthusiastic*, you show *enthusiasm*.

entrepreneur (n.)
a person who starts their own business. An *entrepreneur* sometimes takes *risks* with money.

equality (n.)
when all people are equal and have the same chance to do things

extreme (adj.)
very strong or large in amount. An *extreme* group of people may have very strong opinions that make it difficult for other people to agree with them.

failure (n.)
when someone or something does not succeed

feedback (n.)
an opinion about something that can help you to improve it

filter (n.)
something that removes particular types of light

financial (adj.)
involving or about money

fist (n.)
a hand with the fingers and thumb closed tightly together

fit in (phr. v.)
to belong to a group, plan or situation

freedom (n.)
being free to live as you want and not being controlled by someone

gender (n.)
Your *gender* is if you are a man, a woman, both or neither.

inning (n.)
one of the nine periods of play in a game of baseball

innovative (adj.); **innovate** (v.)
If something is *innovative*, it uses new ideas and methods. To *innovate* is to begin using new ideas and methods.

instant (adj.)
happening immediately.

intuition (n.)
using your feelings to understand
something or to decide what to do

invention (n.); **inventor** (n.)
An *invention* is a new thing that no one
has ever made before. A person who
makes this is an *inventor*.

invest (v.); **investor** (n.)
To *invest* is to put money into
something in order to make more
money. A person who does this is
an *investor.*

Jew (n.)
a person whose religion is Judaism

laser (n.)
A *laser* is a strong piece of light. A
laser printer makes very clear letters
and pictures using a *laser*.

likely (adj.)
probably going to happen

niche (n.)
an activity or job that is right for
a certain person

occupy (v.)
to go into a place and stay there for
a period of time (sometimes to show
that you disagree with something)

order (n.)
the way that a group of people or
things are arranged

original (n.)
an interesting person with new ideas

originality (n.)
the quality of being interesting and
different from all other people or
things

patent (n.)
an official document that allows an
inventor to make or sell their *invention*
for a particular period of time and
prevents anyone else from doing this

personality (n.)
the type of person you are and the
qualities that you have

pitcher (n.)
In baseball, the *pitcher* is the player
who throws the ball at the person
who is going to hit it.

play (n.)
a story written for actors to perform,
usually in a theatre or on the
television or radio

power (n.)
being able to control what happens
or what people do

procrastinate (v.);
procrastinator (n.)
If you *procrastinate,* you wait for
a period of time before doing
something that you must do. A
procrastinator is a person who often
does this.

promote (v.)
to move someone to a higher
position in a company

race (n.)
a group of people who may share
some of the same things, like their
history or parts of what they look like

rebel (n.)
someone who refuses to do what
other people tell them to do

revolutionary (n.)
a person who wants to make
big changes

rights (n.)
the things that everyone must be
allowed to have or do

risk (n.); **risky** (adj.)
If you take *risks*, you do something
even when something bad might
happen because of it. If something is
risky, it involves *risks*.

role model (n.)
a person who behaves in a way that is
a good example for others to follow

status (n.)
someone's position in society because
of their job, the money that they
earn, etc.

suffrage (n.)
being allowed to vote

suggestion (n.)
an idea for people to consider

surface (n.)
the top or outside part of something.
It can describe how someone looks or
seems from the outside.

system (n.)
a way or method of doing something

technology (n.)
facts, ideas and methods from science
that are used to make things

theory (n.)
an idea that tries to explain why
something happens

times (prep.)
to add a number to itself one or more
times. It has the sign x in mathematics.

transportation (n.)
moving people or things from one
place to another

ultrasound (n.)
sound *waves* that can be used to
produce pictures of something inside
your body

wave (n.)
a piece of sound, light, heat or
other energy that travels in a
certain pattern

web browser (n.)
a computer program that allows you
to look at information on the internet

wire (n.)
a long piece of very thin metal. A *wire*
can be covered in plastic and carry
electricity.